# The
# Self-Compassion
# Workbook for BPD

Dialectical Behavior Therapy Skills to
Find Self-Forgiveness, Healing, and Self-Love with
Borderline Personality Disorder

Amanda Smith, LCSW

New Harbinger Publications, Inc.

NEW HARBINGER PUBLICATIONS is a registered trademark of New Harbinger Publications, Inc.

New Harbinger Publications is an employee-owned company.

Copyright © 2025 by Amanda L. Smith
    New Harbinger Publications, Inc.
    5720 Shattuck Avenue
    Oakland, CA 94609
    www.newharbinger.com

All Rights Reserved

Cover design by Amy Shoup

Acquired by Jess O'Brien

Edited by Karen Levy

Library of Congress Cataloging-in-Publication Data on file

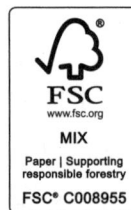

Printed in the United States of America

27  26  25

10  9  8  7  6  5  4  3  2  1      First Printing

"*The Self-Compassion Workbook for BPD* by Amanda Smith is a thoughtful and practical guide for those struggling with borderline personality disorder (BPD). With warmth and insight, Smith tackles the deeply painful experience of self-hatred—a life-changing focus for healing. This workbook offers tools for self-understanding and emotional balance, and can be used alongside dialectical behavior therapy (DBT) and other therapies to support meaningful, lasting change."

—**Karyn Hall**, **PhD**, founder of the Houston DBT Center, certified DBT clinician, coauthor of *The Power of Validation* and *The RO DBT Workbook for Eating Disorders*, and author of *The Emotionally Sensitive Person*

"A much-needed, first-of-its-kind resource for those with BPD seeking to find compassion from within. Grounded in the practice and science of self-compassion, this workbook offers simple yet powerful reflections and guidance to strengthen your self-kindness and support your BPD recovery."

—**Dylan Zambrano**, **MSW**, founder of DBT Virtual, and author of *The DBT Skills Daily Journal*

"Reading this felt like sitting with a kind, knowledgeable therapist who truly gets it. Amanda does an incredible job making DBT and self-compassion feel approachable and real for folks with BPD. I will definitely be recommending this to clients who are working on healing their relationship with themselves."

—**Krisanna Valencia**, **LMSW**, therapist

"It's hard to picture a friend, family member, or client who couldn't benefit from Amanda's guide on self-compassion. Amanda has given us something we all need: a resource that outlines the steps and strategies to loving and supporting our very human and imperfect selves well. For those experiencing life's ups and downs, this will be a resource to cling to and return to again and again for support."

—**Ashton Fisher Jimenez**, **MS, LPC-S**, owner and relationship therapist at Becoming Counseling & Clinical Supervision, board-approved licensed professional counselor supervisor in Texas, and certified eye movement desensitization and reprocessing (EMDR) therapist

"This practical and readable workbook is an achievement of thoughtful integration of the science and practice of self-compassion with those of DBT. Self-compassion is just the right medicine to help people with BPD transform internalized invalidation for a kinder, more integrated relationship with themselves."

—**Scott Spradlin**, **LPC, LMAC**, author of *Don't Let Your Emotions Run Your Life*, and codirector of Wichita DBT at NorthStar Therapy

"Deeply empathic, and illuminated by her extensive experience working with BPD, DBT, and self-compassion, Amanda Smith expertly guides us in recognizing and responding to each moment of suffering as an opportunity to embrace our pain with gentleness and love. Self-compassion is the most powerful means of healing, and Amanda shares these clear, accessible, and powerful practices with the same qualities she helps us nurture within ourselves."

—**Kiera Van Gelder**, **MFA**, author of *The Buddha and the Borderline*

For TD and JS.
Felicis Memoriae

# Contents

# Foreword

Embracing self-compassion facilitates healing of the wounds of those with borderline personality disorder (BPD), but approaching oneself with kindness and empathy may feel elusive or even counterintuitive to people navigating BPD symptoms. Perhaps you were never taught to direct compassion to yourself. Maybe you were unfairly criticized for treating yourself gently or have been accused of being overly sensitive, self-absorbed, or selfish for attempting to care for yourself in this very healthy way. It's no wonder that, given these experiences, you might find the practice of self-compassion impossible or even ludicrous.

Since you have this book in your hands, I think it's a safe bet that either you have realized or someone—perhaps a therapist, friend, or other loved one—has suggested that you struggle with self-compassion and that addressing this could be a powerful step on your healing journey. You want to do everything you can to support your well-being and are looking for a missing key to supplement all of the work you've done to recover and heal. At the same time, you may find the idea of treating yourself with the same compassion, kindness, and empathy that you'd extend to someone you care about a foreign concept. Maybe you can't imagine how you could deserve the act of generating compassion toward yourself or how it could help.

This book is designed to meet you right where you are and help you get to the next phase of your healing journey. It has been written by a therapist who gets you. Amanda L. Smith, LCSW, specializes in borderline personality disorder, self-harm, and dialectical behavior therapy (DBT), which is considered the gold standard of treatment for BPD. I have personally witnessed Amanda compassionately guide those with BPD toward creating and sustaining lives they consider worth living. Her focus on reminding BPD sufferers that their experiences, feelings, and desires matter, are valid, and worth the time and effort of applying self-compassion techniques has had remarkable effects. You will now have the opportunity to experience this firsthand.

Amanda gives you a window into how she has helped countless people with BPD and borderline traits to use the power of self-compassion to radically shift their lives and overcome common obstacles. She includes insights into each of the diagnostic criteria (symptoms) of BPD, including common, relatable ways that these manifest, allowing you to better understand your own experiences. She also includes information on how the concept of self-compassion can be applied to help heal the wounds associated with each BPD symptom. Additionally, each chapter concludes with two case stories of clients with BPD to bring the concepts and application of self-compassionate skills to life. You will find reflections of yourself in many of these case stories, increasing your understanding of your own suffering and helping you gain the perspective and motivation needed to apply self-compassion to your life in truly transformative ways.

Amanda knows that DBT assumes a "skills deficit," meaning that someone with BPD symptoms likely did not learn self-compassion and emotion regulation skills growing up. Often their caregivers didn't know emotional coping skills themselves, making it impossible for them to model such skills. Therefore, in this book, Amanda gives BPD sufferers the opportunity to learn and practice the skills that cultivate self-compassion to help them to grow, change, and heal. She delivers this missing key in a respectful way that honors each reader's unique journey.

Whether you are newly diagnosed with BPD or borderline traits or have been working on your healing for a while now, I'm excited for you. As someone in recovery from borderline personality dis-order myself, who credits embracing self-compassion as a large piece of my healing, I share Amanda's perspective on the importance of self-compassion for people with BPD. The information Amanda shares will likewise help you perceive yourself and your journey in a unique, supportive way. This endeavor is worthwhile, and you will look back at your wise choice to explore this aspect of your healing. Get ready for new insights, breakthroughs, and motivation.

I encourage you to take your time going through this book and responding to the exercises. They will help you get the most out of this book by allowing you to reflect deeply. This book will also help you connect the dots of how an absence of self-compassion has been detrimental to your progress up until now, and how choosing to apply what Amanda teaches you will inevitably and immediately begin to transform your life for the better. You may not believe this yet, but my hope is that you soon will: you deserve this.

In kindness,

—Debbie DeMarco Bennett, MA, (aka Debbie Corso)
Founder of www.emotionallysensitive.com and author of
*Stronger Than BPD*

# Introduction

Congratulations, dear reader! You are about to embark on a long, challenging, and ultimately reward-ing self-compassion adventure.

Have friends or family members ever told you that you are too hard on yourself, that you are your own worst enemy, or that you are someone who could be kinder to yourself? Do you tend to be your own toughest critic? If so, you're not alone. Many people with a diagnosis or traits of borderline per-sonality disorder struggle with self-compassion.

Growing up, you may have been given the message that you need to be "tough" on yourself, and maybe others were also tough on you. While that approach may be beneficial for a lot of people, it may not be helpful for someone with a diagnosis of borderline personality disorder. The goal of this book is to give you self-compassion skills to help improve your life in a way that is in alignment with your goals and values.

My hope is that you will take this book and make it your own by completing each of the skills, exercises, or writing prompts. Your own ideas and perspectives are important as you are learning to increase your capacity to experience and cultivate self-compassion in your life.

Today is not your day to give up or give in. This is the first step in greater awareness of how self-compassion may change your life for the better.

## How to Use This Book

This book is organized according to the *DSM-5* (APA 2013), a manual used by licensed health care professionals to diagnose conditions like depression, anxiety, trauma, and personality disorders, including the criteria for borderline personality disorder. There is a separate chapter for each of the nine diagnostic criteria and a final chapter that recaps a lot of different ideas for people who are strug-gling with their thoughts, emotions, and behaviors.

I want to acknowledge that the *DSM-5* is an imperfect tool for making a diagnosis. In addition, this book is not intended to help you diagnose yourself with any condition. You have probably already noticed that some diagnostic criteria may be a fit for you and others may not. For many people, a diagnosis helps provide a framework to understand themselves. For others, it paints an incomplete picture of who they are or how they experience life.

You, of course, are not defined by a label or a diagnosis in a book. You are a whole person with a unique lived experience, values, talents, and goals. You are an individual who is inherently worthy of healing, recovery, and self-acceptance. My hope is that this book plays a small part in your journey toward the wholeness you were meant to experience in life.

I'm a big believer in the 12-step program wisdom of "take what you need and leave the rest." If there are stories, ideas, exercises, writing prompts, or other suggestions contained in this book that don't apply to you or don't feel like they are a fit for you at this point in your life, that's perfectly okay. You can find a way to implement what works and set aside the ideas that aren't for you.

Another point that I'd love for you to consider is that the psychological concept of willingness or openness (May 1982) is another way for you to benefit from the exercises contained in this book. Sometimes we have moments where we have an urge to automatically reject ideas without understanding how they might be catalysts for learning more about ourselves and others. Keeping an open mind is just one self-compassionate practice that could make a difference for you as you read and complete this book.

Ultimately, this book is for you and my hope is that you will find some wisdom in these pages. Will you allow yourself the opportunity to learn and grow through self-compassion in a way you may not have previously imagined?

## What You Will Learn in This Book

My hope is that you'll learn a lot about yourself and your diagnosis as you take the time to work through this book. Even though you may have read a lot of books and have access to excellent information about borderline personality disorder, I encourage you to take a look at each chapter and use it as an opportunity to review the diagnostic criteria. You'll find specific and practical self-compassion exercises in each chapter. Many of these exercises are also available on the website for this book at http://www.newharbinger.com/55664. Feel free to print them out and use them as many times as needed.

I believe that each distressing emotion, every unwanted thought, and every urge to engage in self-sabotaging or self-harming behaviors is actually a moment when you can use the self-compassion exercises as a way to help yourself cope with your symptoms just a little bit better.

Even if a specific diagnostic criterion doesn't fit or describe your symptoms at this time, you may find that learning about and using an exercise in that chapter may still be beneficial. By working through the entire book, you might find some wisdom and helpful ideas that you hadn't expected. Again, your willingness and open mind will help you determine what will be most helpful when it comes to developing your own self-compassion practice.

A consistent, daily practice will help you build a self-compassion muscle that grows stronger with each effort to be self-compassionate.

Once you complete this book, I believe that you will:

- Have a better understanding of how a self-compassion practice may benefit you

- Identify more opportunities in your life for self-compassion

- Reduce your suffering and emotional pain by creating your own personalized self-compassion practice

To that end, write about what you hope to understand and accomplish once you've completed this book. What is most important to you?

_____

_____

_____

# CHAPTER 1

# What Is Self-Compassion?

Simply put, self-compassion refers to an attitude of kindness, benevolence, and nonjudgmental understanding toward one's self. Self-compassion researcher and author Kristin Neff (2011) notes that much of our emotional pain comes from self-judgment and that we can reduce that emotional pain when we recognize our own suffering. That small moment of awareness can then become a beautiful pause when we allow ourselves to be more compassionate. We might also understand self-compassion as a choice we make to treat ourselves with the same gentleness and warmth that we would show a friend, family member, or even a stranger on the street.

Self-compassion—as a mental health tool—may help us work toward important goals in a self-loving, self-respecting, and self-accepting way. Self-compassion is not an easy way out: it's actually extraordinarily hard work for most people with a diagnosis of borderline personality disorder.

Unfortunately, there are some myths that come up when people talk about being self-compassionate. These myths or false assumptions about self-compassion might include things like:

- Self-compassion is a selfish act.

- Being self-compassionate is a narcissistic or self-absorbed way to think or behave.

- Ambitious, successful people are hard on themselves.

- Self-compassion is too simple to really work.

- Demanding perfection from yourself or others helps you get more of what you want in life.

- In order to heal, you need to toughen up and get real.

- Being self-compassionate means that you'll lose control, and some days all you have is control.

- People who are self-compassionate are more likely to give up or give in.

- Self-compassionate people aren't respected by others.

- People who are self-compassionate are "soft" or "feminine."

- Being self-compassionate means that you aren't working toward change.

If you've had or heard other drawbacks to being self-compassionate, list them below:

_____

_____

_____

You may want to consider that your healing may depend on becoming consistently more self-compassionate. Self-compassion, as a daily practice, may be an important tool as you set and work to achieve important goals. In this way, being harder on yourself may actually inhibit or delay your healing from borderline personality disorder.

The following worksheet provides ideas to think about as you work through this book. If you are unable to answer the questions now, think about returning to this exercise at a later time. You might also find that your answers change as you learn more about developing your own self-compassion practice. This worksheet can also be found at http://www.newharbinger.com/55664.

## Exploring Self-Compassion in Your Life

How do you define self-compassion for yourself? How do you know when you are being self-compassionate?

_____

_____

_____

Do you remember a time in your life when you were self-compassionate and made a decision to be kind to yourself in the face of a mistake, difficult situation, or a crisis? Write about it below.

_____

_____

_____

_____

What are some emotions that come up for you when you notice moments of self-compassion in your life?

_____

_____

_____

What are some of the thoughts you might have when you are being more self-compassionate?

_____

_____

_____

Some people are attuned with how self-compassion feels in their body. If this is true for you, what would you notice?

_____

_____

_____

# Are There Downsides to Being Self-Compassionate?

There are potential downsides, drawbacks, and even risks to any kind of therapy, treatment, or intervention. Many people who start a self-compassion practice experience things like:

- Discomfort around changing thoughts and emotions

- Feelings of fear or doubt, and they may ask themselves, "Will the pros of learning how to become more self-compassionate outweigh the cons?"

- Difficult memories or thoughts about times when they haven't been self-compassionate

- Shame, embarrassment, or guilt when they remember moments in their relationships when they made choices that went against their values or beliefs

- Frustration with themselves when they fall back into old patterns of self-hatred or self-sabotaging behaviors

As with many kinds of effective, evidence-based treatments, we sometimes expect people to temporarily feel worse before they begin to feel better. This is perfectly normal. Remember that not everyone feels happy, fulfilled, or encouraged when they leave their therapist's office, 12-step meeting, or support group. Sometimes we're left asking ourselves even more questions as we struggle through periods of inevitable change in our lives. You may have heard this and I've found that it's definitely true: recovery is neither a linear nor nicely predictable process.

In fact, you may have periods when it seems like nothing is happening. You are doing the work you've set out to do but identifying leaps of progress might feel futile. Again, this is common. Real recovery happens when you take very small steps forward over an extended period of time. For many people, this may mean years or even decades. Recovery requires a lot of patience. You, however, are worthy of this investment in yourself.

If you have any questions about whether this practice is appropriate for you, I encourage you to share your concerns with your therapist, social worker, case manager, peer support provider, psychiatrist, family member, or friend. My hope is that they can provide you with some feedback about how you might benefit from greater self-compassion.

Do you anticipate other obstacles to come up as you develop a practice of becoming self-compassionate? What might they be?

---

---

---

# The Science Behind Self-Compassion

We know that a self-compassion practice can benefit a lot of different people facing a lot of difficult challenges. For instance, greater self-compassion may:

- Help reduce suicide risk after a traumatic event (Liu, Wang, and Wu 2020)

- Mediate shame in individuals with narcissistic personality disorder (Kramer et al. 2018)

- Reduce aggression in individuals with a diagnosis of borderline personality disorder (Sommerfeld and Bitton 2020)

- Be an important intervention for adults with ADHD (Beaton, Sirois, and Milne 2022)

- Provide a protective factor against anxiety (Tali et al. 2023)

- Help decrease rumination (Kirschner et al. 2019)

The explosion in research over the past decade has pointed again and again toward the powerful link between self-compassion and emotional health. Check out the scientific literature for yourself by going to pubmed.gov or scholar.google.com and doing a keyword search for "self-compassion," "self-compassion + borderline personality disorder," "self-compassion + depression," "self-compassion + alcohol use," or other relevant keywords to learn more as new research is published.

Going beyond what's written in this book and learning more about the ways in which self-compassion helps people is another way to keep yourself motivated. You can even share what you learn with others as a way of creating a more self-compassionate world.

# Dialectical Behavior Therapy and Self-Compassion Skills

I was first introduced to the idea of self-compassion when I found Christopher Germer's book called *The Mindful Path to Self-Compassion: Freeing Yourself from Destructive Thoughts and Emotions* (2009). I was already familiar with the concept of mindfulness through the evidence-based work of psychologist Marsha Linehan—creator of dialectical behavior therapy (1993)—and was interested in learning more.

I think that everyone in my life must know that I love dialectical behavior therapy (DBT). DBT has given me practical skills I use every single day. This is something that has helped me both personally and professionally. For the past decade, I've seen how many other people have found healing and hope in using these skills so that they can create, in Marsha Linehan's words, a "life worth living."

If you are not already familiar with DBT, it's a treatment that was developed first for individuals with a diagnosis or for those with traits of borderline personality disorder. Marsha Linehan observed that many people had what she called a "skills deficit" in many different areas of their lives. She had a theory that teaching these missing or underdeveloped skills would help reduce cognitive, emotional, and relational dysfunction in her clients, and it turns out that she was right: for many people, DBT is a highly effective, life-changing treatment.

The good news is that we now know that traditional DBT and adaptations of DBT can help people with a lot of different problems like depression, addiction, eating disorders, and PTSD. It's not just for people with a diagnosis of borderline personality disorder or for those who engage in self-harming behaviors.

Like DBT, self-compassion is fairly simple, but implementing the skills can be difficult. Undoing the automatic "tapes" or thought patterns can be a challenge. Self-compassion is also a good indicator of emotional health, regardless of a particular diagnosis or group of symptoms. That means that people who are emotionally healthier are also more likely to be self-compassionate. Like the DBT skills that many people are familiar with, self-compassion can be thought of as a skill that can be taught and then practiced. Self-compassion is a life skill that can be assessed or measured over time. We can also document our progress in becoming more self-compassionate so that we can self-assess just how helpful self-compassion can be as a mental health tool.

In many ways, DBT and self-compassion go hand in hand. When the second edition of Marsha Linehan's skills training manual was published in 2015, she included a brief section about spiritual mindfulness exercises and wrote about a practice called lovingkindness—a way to be self-compassionate by showing kindness to oneself and others. This further validates the principle that self-compassion can play an important role in how people recover from borderline personality disorder and self-harming behaviors and create a life worth living (Linehan 1993).

It makes sense to approach DBT and DBT skills through the lens of self-compassion. Not only are these ideas complementary but they also work together in a more powerful and effective way. Engaging in DBT skills in a self-compassionate way is something that can make a difference in how you understand and respond to your emotional pain.

Self-compassion practice is also wholly compatible with other excellent treatments for borderline personality disorder, such as mentalization-based treatment, schema-focused therapy, transference-focused treatment, and Systems Training for Emotional Predictability and Problem Solving (STEPPS). If you are working with a therapist who uses attachment theory and specializes in helping people create healthier relationships, increased self-compassion will be an important skill as well. Self-compassion work can also be a life-changing part of recovery from addictions or addictive behaviors.

Because the self-compassion skills contained in this book are a good fit with so many other effective therapies and treatments, I'd like for you to consider that practicing self-compassion can play an important role in your emotional health in whatever therapy or treatment plan you are pursuing.

Before you embark on the rest of this book, complete the following quiz to assess just how self-compassionate you are today. This worksheet can also be found at http://www.newharbinger.com/55664.

# Quiz: How Self-Compassionate Are You?

Rate yourself on a scale of:

0 = this statement rarely or never applies to me

1 = this statement applies to me just a little

2 = this statement applies to me some of the time

3 = this statement applies to me about half the time

4 = this statement applies to me most of the time

5 = this statement almost always applies to me

I don't like myself a lot of the time.                                                    _____

I experience self-disgust.                                                                _____

I spend a lot of time blaming myself for problems that aren't always my responsibility.   _____

My friends have noticed that I'm really hard on myself.                                   _____

I demand a lot of perfection from myself.                                                 _____

I call myself mean names when I'm alone.                                                  _____

Self-acceptance seems more challenging for me than it is for others I know.               _____

I hate myself when I make mistakes.                                                       _____

Sometimes I hurt myself when I think about things I've done or said in the past.          _____

It's hard for me to encourage myself.                                                     _____

A family member, friend, teacher, or boss has said, "You should stop beating             _____
yourself up."

I often imagine that I don't deserve happiness.                                           _____

I judge myself more than I judge others.                                                  _____

It's rare for me to remember moments when I like myself or am proud of my                 _____
accomplishments.

When I'm self-critical, I tend to also be more critical of others.                        _____

I get stuck imagining that my future is pretty hopeless.                                  _____

I spend a lot of time thinking that I should be more like other people.                   _____

I cannot accept myself; I must change who I am.                                           _____

I frequently tell myself that I shouldn't feel the way that I do.                         _____

If I say or do something in a group of people, I'll often want to "redo" what I said      _____
or did.

Add up your total points along with today's date for future reference and reflection.

_____ points on _____.

A higher score (75 to 100 total points) indicates that you may have greater challenges in being self-compassionate. A score below 75 may indicate that you have low or moderate challenges in being self-compassionate and, of course, you still might have some room for improvement.

What did you notice when you were completing this self-assessment?

_____

_____

_____

_____

Is there an opportunity for you to share your responses with a therapist, peer support provider, other helping professional, or a friend? If so, what did they observe about your results? Were they surprised by your answers?

_____

_____

_____

_____

Mindfully observing moments when you are hard on yourself or when you are self-critical is a great first step toward creating change and becoming more self-compassionate. As you learn more and work through this book, I hope that you come back to this exercise and see how far you've come. Making a note of the date will help you assess your progress. Acknowledging growth in this area of your life is another way to practice compassion toward yourself. Any progress counts, so think about how you can reward yourself for making small changes that lead to more self-compassion.

Now that you have a basic understanding of how self-compassion can help you in your journey of healing from borderline personality disorder, you're ready to examine each of the diagnostic criteria in more detail and apply self-compassion skills to that area.

# Summary

- A self-compassion practice may be an important part of healing and recovery for you and others facing similar problems.

- You don't need a particular diagnosis or set of symptoms in order to benefit from becoming more self-compassionate.

- Practicing self-compassion isn't an easy way out of any problem. It can be one of the most challenging but effective ideas that you keep in your mental health toolkit.

- Keeping track of when and how you practice self-compassion may be instrumental in how you increase your capacity to become self-compassionate. The more you practice, the easier it will be to implement these ideas.

# CHAPTER 2

# Frantic Efforts to Avoid (Real or Imagined) Abandonment

As a person with borderline personality disorder, you may sometimes respond with fear to any sense of rejection or abandonment in your important relationships. This may include romantic relationships or relationships with friends, family members, or other people you feel deeply connected to in your life.

Your fear or anxiety does not have to be real or imminent. For instance, sometimes I work with clients who believe that their partner will leave them over a small misunderstanding or argument. Most of the time, these fears seem real but, when we use a dialectical behavior therapy (DBT) skill like Check the Facts (Linehan 2015), we learn that they aren't necessarily true or accurate.

This fear of abandonment might look like:

- "Blowing up" someone's phone with texts or calls when messages have gone unread or phone calls haven't been returned.

- Not allowing someone to physically leave a discussion that has escalated.

- Verbally or physically threatening others when you have been ignored, experienced invalidation, or felt misunderstood.

- Grabbing someone's keys or wallet when they attempt to leave.

- Threatening self-harm or suicide during a break-up or separation.

- Begging or pleading with others to stay with you.

- Insisting that you cannot be left alone.

- Blocking, muting, unfollowing others on social media accounts when you've felt rejected or hurt.

Of course, not everyone with a diagnosis or traits of borderline personality disorder has experienced this symptom, or it might be true that this behavior has only come up for you in relationships that have felt less secure. If you're in healthier relationships with family members, friends, or a romantic partner and have a higher level of trust in those relationships, you may rarely or never feel rejected or abandoned. Complete the following worksheet to assess how prevalent this symptom is for you. This worksheet can also be found at http://www.newharbinger.com/55664.

## Assessing Your Fear of Abandonment

Is this symptom of borderline personality disorder a fit for you? What has been your experience with feeling abandoned or rejected?

_____

_____

_____

_____

_____

How have you reacted to feeling abandoned or rejected?

_____

_____

_____

How might learning self-compassion skills help you with fears of abandonment?

_____

_____

_____

_____

# The Benefits of Self-Compassion When Experiencing Rejection or Abandonment

There are many different ways to practice self-compassion. One of the cornerstones of a self-compassion practice is the idea that we can treat ourselves with the same kindness, thoughtfulness, and consideration that we would use to respond to a friend who is experiencing a similar difficulty, problem, or even a crisis. The following worksheet will help you practice this skill. This worksheet can also be found at http://www.newharbinger.com/55664.

## Exploring Your Compassion for Others

Think about a time when you've supported and encouraged a friend, family member, neighbor, or coworker during a difficult time. Which of the following attributes described you as you were compassionately present for someone you cared about? Check all that apply and feel free to add other descriptors or observations.

| | |
|---|---|
| ☐ nonjudgmental | ☐ encouraging |
| ☐ helpful | ☐ selfless |
| ☐ loving | ☐ validating |
| ☐ wise | ☐ charitable |
| ☐ calm | ☐ honored |
| ☐ valuable | ☐ peaceful |
| ☐ respectful | ☐ connected |
| ☐ gentle | ☐ sensitive |
| ☐ purposeful | ☐ appreciative |
| ☐ courageous | ☐ quiet |
| ☐ empathic | ☐ confident |
| ☐ merciful | ☐ easygoing |
| ☐ careful | ☐ other: _____ |
| ☐ generous | ☐ other: _____ |

What do you think or feel about your experience when you remember a time when you were compassionate, kind, and loving toward a friend, family member, or even an animal?

_____

_____

_____

_____

_____

Pay close attention to the words you checked off and your response to the last question. These words may describe who you are when you are at your very best. They may point to moments when you are not only compassionate with others but also self-compassionate.

We are all connected! Being in relationships means that we are, at times, vulnerable to being hurt, rejected, or misunderstood. For someone with a diagnosis of borderline personality disorder, these moments of real or perceived rejection can be both confusing and painful. Remembering who you are when you like others as well as yourself may help you more clearly understand the moments when connections between you and others are most meaningful to you.

## Self-Compassion Skill: Observing Moments When You Can Choose Self-Compassion

The first self-compassion skill is to mindfully notice moments when you can respond to your emotional pain with kindness, gentleness, and self-compassion. This skill will help improve your relationships as well as be an expression of self-respect. If you know the dialectical behavior therapy (DBT) skills, you can use the skills of mindfully observing and describing (Linehan 2015).

The skill of *mindfully observing* means that we are noticing something:

- With intention

- In the present moment

- Without judgment

We often think that we are observing, but mindful observation is much more than looking around our environment. When we are mindfully observing, we are fully present with that observation, and that may take several quiet minutes of uninterrupted attention. We usually don't mindfully observe in just a moment or two. This is one of those deceptively challenging skills that most of us are guilty of rushing through. We know that we've mindfully observed when we really slow things down long enough to begin to understand what is happening to us or others.

You might say to yourself, "Right now I have a choice that is mine alone to make. I can respond with self-compassion or self-condemnation. Is this a moment for self-compassion?" Slowing down and responding to difficult moments with nonjudgmental awareness is key. This idea will give you the space you need to make wiser, healthier decisions and it will help you stay in control of the behaviors you may want to change.

Of course, you don't need to have all the answers or know just the "perfect" thing to do or say next. All you are doing with this skill is simply asking yourself an important question that may help change your life for the better.

## How to Use This Skill

How often are you just mindfully observing without rushing to describe an emotion, thought, or experience? For most people, it's actually a pretty challenging idea. Using the skill of mindfully observing can take a lot of practice. Here are two ways to practice this skill in daily life:

1.  Intentionally set aside three to five minutes each day to mindfully observe something in your environment (like a book on a table or a bird outside your bedroom window), and then turn your attention to observe something inside of yourself (like a physical sensation, thought, emotion, or urge).

2.  Set several one-minute reminders on your phone, and then when the reminder chimes or rings, stop whatever you are doing so you can mindfully observe something in that present moment.

You might decide to try both strategies and then pick one to use for the next week or ten days. The following worksheet will help you explore how you can incorporate mindful observation into your life. This worksheet can also be found at http://www.newharbinger.com/55664.

# Mindful Observation in Your Own Life

What do you think about observing moments when you can choose self-compassion as a way of helping yourself when you feel rejected, abandoned, or hurt by another person?

_____

_____

_____

Some people are naturally more mindful than others. Is this an idea that comes easily to you or do you need to make a commitment to practicing this DBT skill?

_____

_____

_____

Is it easier for you to mindfully observe things that are happening outside of you (like observing how your cat is sleeping or how your refrigerator makes a quiet humming noise) or inside of you (like your breath, heart rate, a physical sensation, or an emotion)?

_____

_____

_____

Why do you think that Marsha Linehan created this skill? What are the benefits of learning how to mindfully observe a moment when you can choose to be self-compassionate?

_____

_____

_____

# Using Stories as a Way to Learn and Understand Self-Compassion

In each chapter of this book, you'll find two fictional stories that help demonstrate both a diagnostic criterion for borderline personality disorder and a way to approach that symptom—or set of symptoms—with more self-compassion. You may even see parts of yourself in these stories, and a story may help you understand yourself just a little bit better.

After you read each story, you'll find a worksheet to help you think about how that story may apply to your life. My hope is that these stories will be a catalyst for learning more about how you can be self-compassionate while using your DBT skills.

Some of these stories can be difficult to read. If you come across a story that creates a lot of unwanted emotions for you, please feel free to take a break and skip to the next story or another part of this book. If you are currently in treatment, please let your therapist know that a story was difficult for you to read so that you can talk about the experience together.

Not every story contained in this book will apply to every reader. I encourage you to think about what fits for you and challenge yourself to find a way to become more compassionate with yourself when you think about that particular symptom or part of the diagnosis.

Finally, I often feel inspired when I read biographies and memoirs about people who are self-compassionate or have learned to become more self-compassionate. If this sounds like something that may help you, I encourage you to check out Marsha Linehan's memoir titled *Building a Life Worth Living* (2020), where she shares her personal story of recovery from self-harming behaviors and how she developed the DBT skills. You'll even read about how a moment of self-compassion completely changed her life.

## • *Cassie's Story*

*Cassie was a freshman in college when she met her first boyfriend. All of Cassie's friends at school said that she "fell hard" for her boyfriend and, at that time in her life, Cassie thought, "This is what love is. When you love someone, they become your entire world. You might even have to fight for the relationship. It's the two of you against the world." Cassie and her boyfriend were together for about six months when one day, Cassie's boyfriend mentioned that he wanted to transfer to another college almost 300 miles away for his sophomore year. He told Cassie that a long-distance relationship might be hard for both of them and hinted that they may want to break up before he left.*

*In that moment Cassie was shocked by what she was hearing and couldn't speak for several minutes. Her body and mind became numb and she felt like she was no longer a part of the conversation. When her boyfriend stopped speaking a few minutes later, she quickly grabbed his arm, began pulling him toward herself, and through her tears, told him that they would always be* together. She was both confused and frightened by what she was doing. She didn't understand her own emotional reaction and was later horrified to see that she had left a mark on her boyfriend's arm where she held him.

Cassie's boyfriend reassured her in the moment but was also confused and frightened by her surprising reaction. He had never seen this side of Cassie. The next day he broke up with her—just a week before Valentine's Day. Cassie was devastated but was also still confused by her reaction to their conversation. She felt embarrassed and wondered what she had done wrong. She thought that they had a strong relationship. Cassie thought that she might marry her boyfriend one day after they graduated from college. Leaving him to attend another college was the last thing she'd ever do.

Several years later, when Cassie was diagnosed with borderline personality disorder, her therapist heard this story and said, "It sounds like you were feeling abandoned and scared in that moment. Your strong reaction made sense given your serious commitment to the relationship." Her therapist used this story from Cassie's life as a way to help illustrate the first symptom for borderline personality disorder in the DSM-5.

Cassie's therapist then went on to explain that when upsetting memories like this come up for Cassie, she could make a decision. She could respond to those painful moments in a self-compassionate way or she could continue to stay stuck with a lot of unwanted and self-judgmental thoughts ("I'm a bad person for grabbing my boyfriend's arm") or emotions like sadness, shame, guilt, or embarrassment. Cassie's therapist told her that responding to these thoughts and emotions with compassion for herself would reduce the intensity and duration of those thoughts and emotions.

Her therapist emphasized that this was a choice that she could make again and again throughout her life and that choosing to be self-compassionate was a tool that she could use anytime and anywhere to help herself. Self-compassion was something that could empower her. Cassie's therapist went on to explain some of the scientific research supporting self-compassion as an important tool in emotional health. She said, "Emotionally healthy people are people who are more self-compassionate."

To Cassie, the idea of responding to her emotional pain with self-compassion sounded like a foreign language, and yet she was intrigued by the idea of a tool she could use to help herself when difficult memories came up for her. She was open to hearing more from her therapist and said that she was up for the challenge of using her DBT skills of mindfully observing and describing in this new way.

Cassie's therapist explained that, like any new skill, self-compassion is something that can be learned and practiced. She said that the more we practice self-compassion, the more self-compassionate we become. That made sense to Cassie.

Use the following worksheet to reflect on Cassie's story and how it is similar or different from your experience.

# Reflecting on Cassie's Story

What elements of the story resonate with you? Is Cassie's experience familiar to you?

_____

_____

_____

Intrusive or upsetting memories about feeling abandoned or current fears of abandonment are common for many people with a diagnosis of borderline personality disorder. Explore the times when fears of abandonment or separation have been problematic for you in your relationships. These may be past experiences or times when you imagine that fears of abandonment may come up again in the future.

_____

_____

_____

_____

What would it look like for you to consistently treat yourself the way you would respond to a really good friend who was feeling abandoned and looked to you for support?

_____

_____

_____

What is something that gets in the way of treating yourself like a really good friend, a beloved pet, a child, or someone else you really care about?

_____

_____

_____

# Self-Compassion Scripts

A self-compassion script or self-compassion narrative accompanies each fictional story contained in this book. It is a brief narrative statement that helps you remember why you are choosing self-compassion. You can read these scripts out loud, post them on a bathroom mirror to recite each morning, or create a brief voice memo to listen to when you need a reminder to be a little more self-compassionate. A self-compassion script can be general in nature or may focus on something more specific to the problem you are currently facing.

When Cassie's therapist asked her to write a self-compassion script or narrative for this particular memory, she wrote the following statement she could refer back to when needed.

*When I think about this time in my life, I want to remember that I was young and this was my first relationship. I didn't know a lot about being in love and I knew less about myself and my values in a romantic relationship. My reaction at that time in my life makes sense and I've forgiven myself for hurting someone I loved.*

*Since that time, I've learned a lot about myself and can create healthier relationships that are not based in a fear of abandonment or separation. Treating myself like I would treat a good friend helps me when I think about that period of my life several years ago.*

Could you create a similar plan for helping yourself in the future? What would that self-compassion plan look like? What would you want to remember or what could you tell yourself in the moment?

_____

_____

_____

_____

_____

## • *Geoff's Story*

*Geoff is thirty-four years old, married, and has one son who is three years old. Geoff and his wife have been married for five years and, as he describes it, they have always had a tumultuous relationship marked by arguing, yelling, and saying mean things to each other during fights. At times, the verbal display of their mutual anger scared their son to the point where he would hide in his bedroom closet or underneath his bed and cry.*

However, Geoff also described his relationship with his wife as "strong" and "loving" and would frequently tell friends and family members that he wouldn't know what to do without her. They had met in high school but didn't date at that time. Geoff and his wife became reacquainted in their mid-twenties when they met again at a local baseball game that was attended by mutual friends. Together they started a business that grew to twenty employees in just two years. Geoff credited the success of the business to their teamwork as a couple.

After a particularly difficult argument between Geoff and his wife at work, Geoff's wife said to him, "You have to stop blaming me for everything that goes wrong. I don't know how much more I can take. You don't appreciate all that I do here. Sometimes I think that the only way to solve these problems is for me to quit so that you can run this business by yourself." Geoff was shocked and, in front of an employee, grabbed his wife's car keys out of her hand, and yelled, "You aren't leaving. You aren't going anywhere."

A moment later, a manager intervened, grabbed the keys, gave them to Geoff's wife, and said to him, "Hey, it's okay. Let's talk." The manager led Geoff into an empty office where he broke down in tears as soon as the door was closed. He said, "Why did I do that? I can't live without her."

A little over a week later, Geoff and his wife were in the office of a therapist who works with couples who want to strengthen their relationship. The therapist encouraged Geoff and his wife to also see their own individual therapists and they both agreed. It was Geoff's therapist, a psychologist whose practice is dedicated to helping people become more self-compassionate, who told him about borderline personality disorder. Not all of the symptoms were a fit for him, but he recognized that his fear of abandonment and anger problems were the catalyst for taking his wife's keys during the argument. It wasn't the first time Geoff felt out of control in his relationship.

Geoff's therapist defined self-compassion as a skill and helped him understand how it might look in his life. She told him that becoming more self-compassionate would help prevent situations like the one he recently experienced. Geoff admitted that he is often hard on himself and hard on others. He wanted things to be, in his words, "perfect" in his relationship and, when they weren't, he admitted that he could become angry and verbally abusive. Geoff insisted that he wanted to save his marriage and was willing to do anything in order to make that happen.

He said to his therapist, "I don't know what it means to be self-compassionate, but if it means that we'll argue less, I'm ready." Geoff's therapist replied, "I believe in you. Your first step is using your DBT skills of observing mindfully and describing moments when you have a choice to respond to those feelings of rejection or abandonment with self-compassion. I want for you to keep track of those moments this week."

Use the following worksheet to reflect on Geoff's story and how it is similar or different from your experience.

# Reflecting on Geoff's Story

What elements of the story resonate with you? Is Geoff's experience familiar to you?

_____

_____

_____

Geoff's fear of abandonment was sparked when his wife made a comment about quitting their business. Write about the times when fears of abandonment or rejection have come up for you.

_____

_____

_____

_____

Responding to real or imagined fears of rejection with self-compassion and kindness toward yourself is hard work that won't feel natural for most people. If you were Geoff's friend, how would you encourage him to take that first step and make a choice about responding to his emotional pain with self-compassion?

_____

_____

_____

_____

Geoff's therapist encouraged him to write a brief script that could help him reframe moments when he has an urge to act out in anger and respond to his thoughts and emotions with more compassion. His therapist suggested that he read the script to himself at least twice a day for the next thirty days.

*I sometimes become angry and punishing toward the people I love the most. My goal is to improve my relationship with my wife and son. When I become angry and have urges to yell, I can remember that I love them and that they love me. Responding to my emotional pain with self-kindness helps me but is also a way for me to show my love for them. Yelling is a choice I don't have to make.*

Is there anything else you could imagine Geoff adding? What else might be important for Geoff to remember? Write or edit the script below.

_____

_____

_____

_____

_____

_____

_____

_____

# Summary

- Self-compassion is a purposeful, active choice you make to help yourself.

- Using the DBT skill of mindfully observing is an effective way for you to find moments when self-compassion may help.

- Mindfully observing isn't a race. It doesn't happen in just a moment or two. You may need to slow things down to understand your emotional responses and the choices in front of you.

- Creating a personalized self-compassion practice is extraordinarily hard work. Don't allow yourself to get sidetracked by perfectionism.

- A self-compassion script is a way to remind yourself that responding to your emotional pain with self-compassion is a healthy choice.

Add your own ideas below.

- _____

- _____

# CHAPTER 3

# A History of Unstable and Dysfunctional Relationships

Have you ever wondered why you might feel connected and caring toward a friend one day and then be dismissive of them or even mean to them the next day? People with borderline personality disorder often have a history of challenging relationships. You might have a tendency to either idealize or diminish other people in your life.

If you've ever been friends with someone who liked you one day and seemed cold the next day, you already know how hurtful this relational pattern can be for people with borderline personality disorder. If you don't know exactly where you stand in a relationship or feel threatened by another person, you might also have an urge to treat someone one way and then another based on a strong emotion, misunderstanding, or hurt feelings.

Complete the following worksheet to assess how prevalent this symptom is for you. This worksheet can also be found at http://www.newharbinger.com/55664.

# Assessing Unstable or Dysfunctional Relationships

Is this symptom of borderline personality disorder a fit for you? What has been your experience with difficult or challenging relationships in your life?

_____

_____

_____

_____

_____

Is creating healthier relationships with others an important goal for you? If so, how?

_____

_____

_____

_____

How could increased self-compassion improve your relationships with others?

_____

_____

_____

_____

# Self-Compassion Skill: Validating How Your Thoughts and Emotions Make Sense

We all want to understand ourselves and others. It's an important part of being a healthy person as well as part of a healthy relationship. The second self-compassion skill of *self-validating* is all about recognizing moments when your thoughts and emotions make sense. If you are familiar with DBT skills, you can use the V(alidate) in the GIVE interpersonal effectiveness skill to help improve your relationships with others, but it's also true that you can validate yourself as a way of becoming more self-compassionate (Linehan 2015).

When we are validated by others, we feel acknowledged, connected, and often understood. You may already be receiving validation from others—from a therapist, family member, work colleague, or friend—but how often are you pausing long enough to recognize that you can validate yourself with a sentence like, "It makes sense that I…"? People who are self-compassionate are often self-validating.

Moments where you feel hurt in relationships can be another good opportunity to practice self-compassion. In this way, self-compassion is a powerful practice that can help create better and healthier relationships.

Learning to connect your thoughts and emotions to your behaviors helps you make sense of those hurt feelings you sometimes experience in relationships. This self-compassion practice is a way to communicate to yourself and others that you understand how emotions, thoughts, and behaviors create or influence other emotions, thoughts, and behaviors.

I like to start a sentence with, "It makes sense…" as a way of showing how these connections work. It might sound like this:

- It makes sense that I felt worried; Tomas didn't text back when he said he would.

- It makes sense that I'm grumpy this afternoon; I got less than six hours of sleep last night.

- It makes sense that I'm hungry; I haven't eaten since this morning.

- It makes sense that life is difficult right now; I'm taking five classes this semester and am working fifteen hours a week.

- It makes sense that I'm looking forward to the weekend; I can't wait to relax on Saturday afternoon.

- It makes sense that I feel sad; I'm missing my friends over summer break.

- It makes sense that I'm in love; I'm with someone who likes me just the way I am.

- It makes sense that I'm having a good day; it's my birthday and I received some fun gifts.

Now I'd love for you to connect the dots in a similar way using the following worksheet. This worksheet can also be found at http://www.newharbinger.com/55664.

# Connecting the Dots: It Makes Sense...

Use the following sentence prompts to practice connecting your thoughts, emotions, and experiences with a cause.

It makes sense that today is rough; ... _____

_____

It makes sense that I feel angry; ... _____

_____

It makes sense that I feel happy; ... _____

_____

It makes sense that I am lonely; ... _____

_____

It makes sense that I feel loved; ... _____

_____

It makes sense that relationships can be confusing; ... _____

_____

It makes sense that making friends can be hard; ... _____

_____

Add a few of your own examples in the space below. As you are creating your own examples, see if you can be just a little self-compassionate. Talk to yourself the way you would speak with a friend, your younger self, or someone else you love.

It makes sense that _____(fill in this blank);

_____

_____

It makes sense that _____(fill in this blank);

_____

_____

It makes sense that _____(fill in this blank);

_____

_____

## How to Use This Skill

The compassion we give to others is validating for them. Why wouldn't it be a self-compassionate act for us to validate ourselves?

Sometimes people make the mistake of waiting to be validated by others. The problem with that strategy is that people may not know that you need validating or they may not be able to validate you in the way you'd like. While it's nice to be validated by others, you can take action and get started when you validate your own thoughts and emotions.

Think about how often you are prioritizing self-validation as a way to become more self-compassionate. Are you using this idea once a day or once a week? In chapter 2, I wrote about intentionally setting aside time to use the skill of mindfully observing. This is another way to help you implement this skill. In addition, the following worksheet will help you explore the idea of self-validation in your life. This worksheet can also be found at http://www.newharbinger.com/55664.

# Exploring Self-Validation

What do you think about using a statement like "It makes sense that I..." as a catalyst for self-compassion?

_____

_____

_____

What would help you prioritize self-validation in your life?

_____

_____

_____

Do you know anyone, maybe a friend or a family member, who consistently self-validates? Do you think that is easy or difficult for them?

_____

_____

_____

## • *JT's Story*

*JT is the oldest of three children. He grew up in a one-parent home and found that he often had to take on the role of a protector and provider to his younger brother and sister when their mom would leave their home and use drugs or alcohol with strangers. JT felt a lot of responsibility for keeping his siblings safe. When he was in the fifth grade, a teacher remarked that he always seemed anxious in the classroom. JT remembered that his worry was often tied to a fear that his brother and sister weren't safe unless he was with them.*

*JT did well in school and consistently got As and Bs. When he was in high school, he started taking advanced placement courses and found that he got a lot of fulfillment in learning. He was especially interested in his math classes and loved solving logic puzzles.*

*Making and keeping friends, however, was harder for JT. He seemed to make friends quickly but then something would happen. There would be a miscommunication or misunderstanding and JT would get angry and end the friendship. He spent a lot of time wondering whether other people were trustworthy and admitted that he sometimes looked for reasons to reject friends if they didn't live up to his expectations of what he thought a friend should be. JT didn't have a clear understanding about why this would happen so frequently. He often felt very lonely and it was frustrating to him that he didn't have more friends.*

*When JT went to college he quickly found a friend group in the school's math department. He admired his new friends and felt like he met his intellectual match in this group of guys. JT thought that he finally found some friends he'd be connected to until graduation and maybe even years later.*

*Just a week later, the group decided to go to a concert together and JT was excited about joining in. He offered to buy the tickets for the group and it was agreed that the others would reimburse JT for their ticket. When JT didn't get reimbursed by one friend after a few days, he began to think that maybe the friend was trying to take advantage of JT's generosity and wouldn't pay him back for the concert ticket. Someone he was excited about being friends with a few days ago quickly became an enemy.*

*The next day, JT lashed out at the friend via a group chat and then was reimbursed by that friend about ten minutes later with an apology. JT was a little embarrassed by his strong reaction but also felt justified in his anger. For a short time, he convinced himself that he made a mistake in trying to be friends with guys in this group and even considered leaving college over the incident.*

*JT soon became connected to a therapist on his college campus who talked to him about borderline personality disorder and, in particular, having unstable, intense relationships with a history of liking others and then sometimes rejecting those same people when they had done something where he'd felt wronged or hurt. The therapist explained that liking and then rejecting others can be an exhausting pattern in a relationship. The truth is that people are not all good or all bad. Most people most of the time are doing their best. People who are potentially more sensitive to rejection—like individuals with a diagnosis of borderline personality disorder—may be looking for signals that they will be hurt where none actually exist. The therapist wondered if JT had observed this pattern in his life. JT responded by saying, "I know that I'm pretty hard on people. Sometimes I think that it's easier if I reject others before they hurt me. Maybe I did that again. I just don't know."*

*JT's therapist encouraged him to practice being self-compassionate about being hurt in this friendship by understanding why the fear of being taken advantage of by others made sense. She taught him the "It makes sense that I feel …" or "It makes sense that I think …" statement and they practiced it together around other similar patterns of idealization and devaluation in JT's life.*

*After practicing for a few weeks, JT said that he was feeling a little more compassionate toward himself and less hurt by what happened with his new friend. JT said that this self-compassion skill was something he was willing to practice to see whether it continued to help him manage his emotions with friends.*

Use the following worksheet to reflect on JT's story and how it is similar or different from your experience.

## Reflecting on JT's Story

What elements of the story resonate with you? Is JT's experience in sometimes idealizing and devaluing others familiar to you?

_____

_____

_____

Do you think that JT may be looking for signals that he will be hurt where none actually exist? As a self-compassionate person extending compassion to another individual, what wisdom would you share with him?

_____

_____

_____

When has the pattern of idealizing and then rejecting people come up for you in your friendships or with family members, with someone in your peer group, in the classroom, or with work colleagues?

_____

_____

_____

What would it look like for you to understand these behaviors through a self-compassionate lens?

_____

_____

_____

What is something that gets in the way of understanding how your thoughts, emotions, and behaviors make sense?

_____

_____

_____

When JT's therapist asked him to write a self-compassion script or narrative for this particular diagnostic criterion, he wrote the following self-compassion script he could refer back to when needed.

> *I've always had a difficult time making friends and trusting others. It makes sense that I feel lonely; I want more friends but often feel threatened when misunderstandings come up in relationships. I've learned that I can't always trust my emotions—even when they seem real.*
>
> *Being more self-compassionate allows me to remember that there's a reason why I feel the way I do. There isn't always a threat in my relationships. I don't have to act on my fear and lash out at others. My self-compassion practice allows me to understand myself better.*

Could you create a plan for helping yourself in the future, and what would that self-compassion plan look like? What would you want to remember or what could you tell yourself in the moment?

_____

_____

_____

_____

_____

_____

## • *Cara's Story*

Cara came from a big family and always had lots of siblings and cousins to play with at home. Almost every weekend was filled with fun activities that ended on Sunday night with a big family dinner that was often attended by at least a dozen family members. She felt safe and loved by her parents, grandparents, aunts, and uncles.

The summer she turned sixteen years old, her family moved far away from the rural town where she grew up. When she started school in the fall, she found it very hard to make friends. Cara felt awkward around others at school and began to feel depressed. She told her parents that she wanted to be homeschooled and didn't want to make friends in the new community. She'd spend many hours alone reading and writing stories about her life when she was younger.

Eventually Cara made one friend at a local nonprofit organization where she volunteered on Saturday mornings. This friend became her only friend and was soon her entire world. She wanted to spend every day with this friend and together they started to plan where they would live and work when they both turned eighteen. Cara's parents encouraged her to make other friends but Cara refused. She insisted that this was the only friend she would ever need.

Shortly after they graduated from high school, Cara's best friend met a guy at work and they began to date. At first, Cara was supportive and happy for her best friend but, after a few months, she became jealous and simultaneously protective of her friend. She started judging the boyfriend, made fun of the way he spoke, and then started to talk about how they would eventually break up when she found someone better. Cara's friend found this very hurtful and told Cara. Cara responded by saying, "You never cared about me. I trusted you and you chose him over me."

Within a few months, Cara started to see a therapist who talked to her about how it can be confusing for us and others when we feel so deeply connected to people but then also feel threatened in those relationships. Cara admitted that she missed her friend but was afraid to get close to her again. She said that she didn't want to be hurt by the person she cared about the most. She didn't like feeling vulnerable.

Cara's therapist said, "Of course you don't want to be hurt. You feel things so deeply and this relationship has meant so much to you!"

Together Cara and her therapist worked on the skill of becoming more self-compassionate when she felt confused, insecure, lonely, or threatened in her relationships. The therapist taught her the "It makes sense that I feel …" or "It makes sense that I think …" practice and Cara found that it was a tool that helped her feel just a little bit better.

Use the following worksheet to reflect on Cara's story and how it is similar or different from your experience.

# Reflecting on Cara's Story

What elements of Cara's story resonate with you? Is her experience familiar to you?

_____

_____

_____

How could using the "It makes sense that I..." narrative help Cara self-compassionately respond to her emotional pain of feeling distant from her best friend after she started to date?

_____

_____

_____

Practicing this self-compassion skill might be challenging for a lot of people. What advice do you have for someone who wants to practice this skill regularly? What would help you remember to practice these skills several times a week?

_____

_____

_____

When Cara's therapist asked her to write a self-compassion script or narrative with the "It makes sense that I …" sentence, she wrote the following statement she could refer back to when needed.

_This friendship has meant everything to me over the past two years and it makes sense that I got scared when things changed._

_When I get scared in the future, I can respond by being kind to myself and remembering that there is a reason why I feel the way I do. Self-compassion is a skill I can use to help myself._

What do you think about Cara's self-compassion script? How else could Cara use the "It makes sense that I…" idea?

_____

_____

_____

_____

_____

## Summary

- We can validate others (like friends, family members, or work colleagues) but we can also validate our own thoughts, emotions, or experiences.

- Self-validation means that we acknowledge how our own thoughts, emotions, experiences, urges, goals, and preferences make sense to us.

- Recognizing how a thought or emotion "makes sense" is one way for us to validate ourselves and practice self-compassion.

- You don't need to wait for others to validate you when you can validate yourself.

- The more we practice these ideas, the easier they become.

Add your own ideas below.

- _____

- _____

# CHAPTER 4

# Inconsistent Self-Image or Sense of Self

Understanding ourselves can be challenging. Understanding ourselves within our relationships can be even more difficult. You are not alone if you've ever thought, "I just don't know who I am." Complete the following worksheet to assess how prevalent this symptom is for you. This worksheet can also be found at http://www.newharbinger.com/55664.

## Assessing Self-Identity Challenges

Have you thought or said any of the following? Check all that apply.

☐ *I don't fit in at school/work/home.*

☐ *I don't know what I like or dislike.*

☐ *I don't know who I need to be for others to like or accept me.*

☐ *I change my values depending on whom I'm with that day.*

☐ *I need to be someone I'm not if I expect to be loved.*

☐ *I need to be like others so that I'm not rejected.*

☐ *I change my appearance or how I dress when I'm trying to please others.*

☐ *I always ask many people what I should do before I make an important decision.*

☐ *I allow others to tell me who I am or what I like.*

☐ *I learn about something new and then it becomes an all-consuming passion for me for a short period of time.*

☐ *I try to find other people on social media (YouTube, Facebook, X, Instagram), in TV shows, and in films who can help me understand myself.*

☐ *I feel like I need someone's permission to just be myself.*

☐ *I don't live up to my own expectations but I don't know what "good enough" would look like.*

☐ *Others have told me that I often seem like a different person depending on whom I'm with in the moment.*

☐ *My goals, values, and interests significantly change every few months.*

If you marked several indicators above, that's okay. It's common for most teens and young adults to want to understand who they are within the context of a friend, school, or work group. Fitting in can be a positive experience when other people are learning more about themselves. It's also a way for us to know that there are other people like us with similar values, preferences, and similarities.

People with a diagnosis of borderline personality disorder may often find that they have interests, hobbies, or goals that frequently change based on whom they are with at the moment and what those other individuals may like or not like. Other individuals with the diagnosis may not be able to define who they are or what they like in a way that feels authentic or accurate.

If this describes you, you might find yourself thinking, "I have to be different," and tell yourself, "I won't fit in unless I'm like others in my friend group." It can be a profoundly painful experience when individuals with borderline personality disorder don't know who they are or who they think they should be.

The truth is that you are a multidimensional person with many different parts of yourself. Accepting this fact may be an important part of your healing and recovery from borderline personality disorder.

# Self-Compassion Skill: Self-Acceptance Instead of Change

Like many therapists, I frequently talk to my clients about things in their life that they may want to change. This focus on change might mean that I help my clients change things about themselves that they want to change as part of the goals they want to accomplish in treatment. However, it's also true that many people who come to therapy prefer to focus on what we call acceptance, or what Marsha Linehan refers to as the skill of *radical acceptance*—acceptance that she defines as total, whole, or complete—as one way that they can become more self-compassionate (Linehan 2015). While there is nothing wrong with working toward change, many people with a diagnosis of borderline personality disorder may benefit from creating a goal of developing greater acceptance of themselves.

Focusing on what makes you who you are can be a source of strength. It's here where you communicate to yourself, "This is who I am." Radical acceptance is a distress tolerance skill that helps you accept the things about yourself and others that you may not want to accept, and it can also help you become more self-accepting. You might have a preference about what you need most in the moment. You can choose to:

- Focus on change

or

- Focus on acceptance

You can always choose to focus on both acceptance and change in treatment, weighing the pros and cons of both choices.

Prioritizing acceptance skills helps many people. Of course, there's no right or wrong answer about how you could prioritize acceptance. You may have reasons to be more accepting of yourself and others and there also may be lots of reasons why you want to focus on change. You alone get to decide which skills might help you the most.

Of course, no one can make this decision for you. Even though other people in your life may have opinions or preferences about what they think you should do or how you should act, you are in charge of how you practice these skills. You can find ways to make them uniquely your own.

As I've noted, it is common for people with borderline personality disorder to have an unstable self-image. Self-acceptance can be a way to increase your compassionate understanding of yourself and who you are. When you understand yourself more, you will find that your self-worth and confidence increase. The following worksheet will help you assess how much self-acceptance you have in your life. This worksheet can also be found at http://www.newharbinger.com/55664.

# Exploring Self-Acceptance

Explore three things about yourself or parts of your life that are easier for you to like or accept. For instance, you might want to focus on attributes that you like about yourself. Perhaps you are kind, forgiving, or a loyal friend and you could write about that. If you have a particular natural talent or gift, you might reflect about that part of yourself.

1. _____

_____

2. _____

_____

3. _____

_____

What are the parts of yourself you don't want to change?

_____

_____

_____

What role could self-acceptance play in your healing from borderline personality disorder?

_____

_____

_____

Finding moments to practice self-acceptance is another way you can balance acceptance and change. What could this look like for you on a typical day?

_____

_____

_____

## How to Use This Skill

Over many years, I've found that self-compassionate people find lots of different ways to balance both change and acceptance in their lives. Self-acceptance is very much a choose-your-own-adventure way of becoming more self-compassionate. You are in control of how you use this skill to help yourself. Here are a few examples of how you could use self-acceptance as a way to practice self-compassion.

- You might decide to make a list of the things you can change in your life and the things you cannot change. "Letting go" of the things you can't change can be a sign of acceptance or self-acceptance.

- You might accept that you are doing the best you can and don't need to aim for perfection.

- You could decide that you are "okay" or "fine" just the way you are today.

- You might decide to work on self-acceptance and think about how greater self-acceptance may help you like yourself a little bit more.

- You could accept that you don't always have to fit in with others.

- You could accept that sometimes it might make sense to blend in with the crowd while other times you might prefer to be different.

- You might weigh the pros and cons of accepting yourself exactly the way you are today.

- You might accept that you don't need anyone else's permission to be uniquely you.

## • *Hannah's Story*

*Hannah was about two months into her first semester at college when she first realized that she didn't really know who she was, what she valued, and why her goals were important to her. She had graduated from a fairly small high school and felt lost in a big school almost a thousand miles from the town where she grew up. Her experiences with new friends, classes, and fun activities each weekend were both exciting and overwhelming. Late one evening after a party, she confided in one roommate, "I feel like I don't even know who I am right now. I'm wondering who the real me is: the 'me' from earlier this year when I was still living at home with my parents or the 'me' now."*

*By the end of the semester, Hannah began to experience some depression. It was hard to get out of bed in the morning, she had little energy to get through her classes, her self-confidence took a hit, and she kept thinking, "I just don't fit in here." One of her roommates observed that she had changed since the beginning of the semester and said, "You were so excited when you moved in. That spark is gone. What happened?" Hannah admitted that she wasn't certain what had changed.*

*When Hannah returned to school for the spring semester, she received an email from her school's counseling center about a DBT skills training group that sounded interesting. Hannah spoke with her best friend about the group and she encouraged Hannah to give it a try. The friend* reasoned that it might help her manage her depressive symptoms as well as stay on track with her academic goals. Hannah thought that if she found that it wasn't for her she could just try some other kind of treatment.

Hannah quickly found that DBT was really practical and didn't feel like any other therapy or treatment she had been to in high school. The ideas resonated with her and each week she left group with a skill or an idea that she could use to help herself. She also really liked the two graduate students who led the group. One afternoon, they talked a lot about the role of using DBT skills like radical acceptance along with self-compassion as a way for many students to create some emotional resilience that could provide a buffer against depression and anxiety.

When one of the graduate students announced that she had an opening for individual therapy, Hannah quickly made an appointment. She shared her story and talked about the depression she experienced during her first semester. Hannah said that she believed that something must be wrong with her because she felt like she was becoming a different person in college. That difference created a lot of sad emotions for her.

Hannah also told her therapist that she often felt an internal pressure to be different or that she thought she should be a different person so that other people would like her. She explained that she wanted to fit in but felt like an outsider a lot of the time. Hannah hadn't yet considered that she could accept herself the way she was as a way to be self-compassionate. She wasn't certain what it would mean for her to practice self-compassion by being more self-accepting, but the idea gave her some hope for her future.

A week later, her therapist explained, "It's okay to change the things about your life that you want to change, but there are parts of yourself that you may want to work on accepting. For instance, you may choose to accept that you are a person who is still figuring out who they are at college. It's okay for you to be developing your own interests. You could think about how you are a work in progress and give yourself permission to figure it all out over a long period of time."

That next week, Hannah practiced the skill of radical acceptance each day by observing moments when she was judging herself by entertaining thoughts that she "should" be different or be someone other than who she was during this time of her life. She noticed that this simple observation consistently helped her be more self-compassionate on days when she felt discouraged.

After her next therapy appointment, Hannah wrote "radical acceptance + self-compassion = healthy me" in the notebook she journaled in after each session.

Use the following worksheet to reflect on Hannah's story and how it is similar or different from your experience.

# Reflecting on Hannah's Story

What elements of Hannah's story resonate with you? Is her experience familiar to you?

_____

_____

_____

Are there parts of you or your life that you want to accept and parts of you or your life that you want to change? What are they?

_____

_____

_____

What are the pros and cons of greater self-acceptance in your life?

Pros:

_____

_____

_____

Cons:

_____

_____

_____

Do you have friends, family members, or other people in your life who accept themselves just the way they are? Why do you think self-acceptance is easier for some people?

_____

_____

_____

What do you think about the idea that self-compassion and the skill of radical acceptance can work together to help people heal and grow? Do you have any examples from your own life?

_____

_____

_____

What is something that gets in the way of accepting parts of yourself?

_____

_____

_____

When Hannah's therapist asked her to write a self-compassion script or narrative about how radical acceptance might help her in the future, she thought about how greater acceptance could free her from many of the depressive symptoms she experienced that first semester of school. She wrote:

*Moving from high school to college was such a big change for me. I felt like I needed to change who I was or had to reject parts of me that didn't seem to fit with my new life. There were many times when I thought something was wrong with me because I didn't understand my own interests, values, and what I liked. I didn't know who I was and felt a lot of fear because of the many changes in my life.*

*Becoming more self-compassionate and accepting of who I am can help me manage sad emotions when they come up. I can radically accept that I'm still learning who I am and what I like while understanding how to use self-compassion as a tool to help myself.*

When you think about Hannah's self-compassion script, do you have any additional wisdom to share? What do you think about the idea that acceptance may help her manage her unwanted emotions?

_____

_____

_____

## • *Timothy's Story*

*Timothy was diagnosed with borderline personality disorder when he was twenty-seven years old and was in residential treatment for alcohol use disorder.*

*In treatment he laughed the first time he heard the Serenity Prayer at a 12-step meeting:*

God grant me the serenity to accept the things I cannot change,

courage to change the things I can,

and wisdom to know the difference.

—Attributed to Reinhold Niebuhr (1892–1971)

*He later told his counselor, "I don't know what it means to accept the things I cannot change. That's why I drink. I cannot accept my past. Alcohol gives me a break from my thoughts. Thinking about the past is painful, and I don't want to be in pain."*

*He went on to explain, "I can't accept the things I've done and all the hurt I've caused. I can't accept the things that have been done to me. I'm so far away from myself that I don't even know who I am when I'm sober. Acceptance isn't for me."*

*Timothy's counselor validated his sadness and told Timothy that he didn't believe that reciting a few words at a meeting would take away all of the emotional suffering he experienced in his life. Instead, the counselor encouraged Timothy to keep an open mind about how more acceptance could be an important part of his healing.*

*For homework one day, Timothy's counselor asked him to create a list of all of the things in his life he could change and then make a list of the things he would not change—including his past mistakes or the harm that was done to him. Timothy took the homework assignment seriously and wrote for almost two hours. For the first time in his life, he began to understand that maybe there was room for some acceptance in his life. The next time he heard the Serenity Prayer at a 12-step meeting, he had a different reaction that wasn't quite so dismissive.*

*During his time in treatment, Timothy's counselor continued to talk about the role of self-compassion and acceptance as a part of his recovery from borderline personality disorder and alcohol use disorder. One day he asked Timothy, "Do you think that you'd even be in treatment if you learned about self-compassion and acceptance when you were younger?" Timothy didn't know the answer to that question, but it gave him something to think about as he continued to learn more about how he could live without alcohol.*

*Timothy left treatment with a relapse prevention plan he created with his counselor that included a note about reciting the Serenity Prayer to himself once a day or when urges to use alcohol to cope with his unwanted thoughts or emotions were particularly strong.*

Use the following worksheet to reflect on Timothy's story and how it is similar or different from your experience.

## Reflecting on Timothy's Story

Most people don't spend a lot of time thinking about the things that they can or cannot control in their lives. Consider Timothy's homework exercise. What would your list look like? Could you share this list with a therapist, peer support provider, friend, or 12-step sponsor?

Things I can change:

_____

_____

_____

Things I cannot change:

_____

_____

_____

Practicing greater acceptance about ourselves, others, and our past is extraordinarily difficult. What advice do you have for someone who wants to practice this skill regularly? What would help you remember to practice the skill of radical acceptance?

_____

_____

_____

What would your life be like if you could be more accepting? What would you want to remember or what could you tell yourself when you have an urge to reject parts of yourself you don't like?

_____

_____

_____

Timothy's therapist encouraged him to create a self-compassion script as part of his relapse prevention plan. He wrote:

> *Alcohol doesn't help me be who I was meant to be. Being kind to myself gives me a moment to choose something other than alcohol as a way of dealing with my problems.*
>
> *I will remember that there are things I can control and things I cannot control in my life. I have the wisdom to know the difference between the two. Radical acceptance is a skill that can help me.*

What do you think about Timothy's self-compassion script? Do you have any other ideas that might help him as he tries to rebuild his life without alcohol?

_____

_____

_____

_____

_____

# Summary

- Each day you can choose acceptance or change to create the life you want. There are pros and cons of focusing on change just as there are pros and cons of choosing greater acceptance.

- While there are legitimate reasons to change or be different, you might decide to accept yourself the way you are.

- There are things you can control in life and things you cannot control in life.

- Choosing acceptance, or using the DBT skill of radical acceptance, is a way to become more self-compassionate.

- Working toward becoming a more self-compassionate person as you heal and grow is a way to honor both acceptance and change.

- You, alone, get to decide which skills might help you the most.

Add your own ideas below.

- _____

- _____

# CHAPTER 5

# Impulsive Urges and Behaviors

People with borderline personality disorder can often be impulsive. Sometimes these impulsive behaviors can do damage to a person's relationships, finances, work, and school life. The consequences of impulsive behaviors can also lead to legal consequences, fines, jail, or prison.

Here is a short list of impulsive behaviors that therapists might assess when diagnosing someone with borderline personality disorder:

- Driving fast, aggressively, or recklessly

- Destroying public or private property

- Quitting a job prematurely

- Spending money mindlessly

- Engaging in eating disordered behaviors

- Taking risks that may result in physical harm or even death

- Having sex with strangers

- Skipping class or missing work

- Stalking

- Gambling

- Shoplifting

- Starting fights with strangers

- Arguing with the people you love the most

- Lying

The following worksheet will help you assess whether impulsive behaviors are a problem for you. This worksheet can also be found at http://www.newharbinger.com/55664.

## Assessing Your Impulsive Urges and Behaviors

Is this symptom of borderline personality disorder a fit for you? How have impulsive behaviors affected your life?

_____

_____

_____

Does the list of impulsive behaviors sound like anything you currently experience or have experienced in the past? What else can you add to the list?

_____

_____

_____

What impulsive behaviors have been most challenging for you?

_____

_____

_____

# Damaging Behavior or Joyful Spontaneity?

Not all impulsive behaviors are maladaptive or harmful, nor can every impulsive action be defined as a self-sabotaging behavior.

Both impulsive and spontaneous behaviors may feel fun, enjoyable, and even freeing. When I am helping clients assess for impulsive behaviors that could be potentially damaging or sabotaging, I ask, "What are all the possible consequences of engaging in this behavior?" The more outcomes the client generates, the better. More information means that together we have a clearer picture of choices that could be problematic.

For each of the following situations, indicate whether you think the scenario could be a potentially damaging behavior or a fun behavior that is harmless and part of a life worth living.

IB = Impulsive Behavior That's Potentially Harmful

LF = Life Worth Living Fun

| | |
|---|---|
| Your roommate texts you at 12:30 a.m. to say, "I just got a raise today. Let's go out and celebrate now." You have a breakfast meeting with an important client at 8:30 a.m. It takes you twenty minutes to get ready, and then you're out the door to join her. | IB<br><br>LF |
| The person driving in front of you is going five miles under the speed limit and now you'll be late for a concert. After another mile, you finally have an opportunity to pass them. You lower your window, honk your horn, wave, and sarcastically yell, "Have a great day, friend!" | IB<br><br>LF |
| You take your younger niece out to dinner to celebrate her high school graduation and decide that you'll only have two glasses of wine with dinner. When the server comes back to take your order for dessert, he asks, "Would you like another glass of wine?" and you say, "Sure! Why not?" | IB<br><br>LF |
| You make a mistake at work and your boss says, "Please be more careful next time." You quickly respond by laughing and jokingly say, "Don't worry. You can fire me. I already hate myself more than you ever could." | IB<br><br>LF |
| A friend asks you to stop making fun of an unfortunate haircut she recently got and you immediately make one last joke. When she becomes upset, you say, "It's not a big deal. Stop being so sensitive." | IB<br><br>LF |
| Your girlfriend calls you at 7:00 a.m. and urges you to skip work so that you can both go to the lake on what should be a beautiful day. You have some paid time off you can use, have no meetings scheduled that day, and decide that you'll call in "sick" and join her. | IB<br><br>LF |
| You've had three speeding tickets in the past eighteen months and get pulled over again for speeding. The law enforcement officer asks whether there's an emergency and you quickly make up a story about your mom getting out of the hospital that day to see if you can get away with just a warning. | IB<br><br>LF |
| You go into work early one day, suddenly decide to leave at noon, and join a video call with a coworker from the beach at 3:00 p.m. Your colleague sees where you are and says, "That's a great idea. I should join you next time." | IB<br><br>LF |

| | |
|---|---|
| A friend asks you to be his "plus one" at a wedding reception and you gladly accept, but the next day, another friend asks you to go to a Broadway play for the same night as the wedding. You text your friend who asked you to the wedding reception, explain the situation, and say, "I know you'll understand why I can't go with you." | IB<br><br>LF |
| It's early in the semester but you cut class to meet a friend for coffee who needs your help with a relationship problem. Later that day, you email your professor telling him about your friend's problem and letting him know that you'll be back in class next week. | IB<br><br>LF |

# Self-Compassion Skill: Giving Yourself Time to Make Healthy Decisions

Life is full of distressing moments and situations. It's important to acknowledge that we don't always need to act on our feelings of distress. In fact, it is better to be able to sit with, or tolerate, distressing feelings without doing or saying something that will make it worse. Marsha Linehan explains that the distress tolerance skill *STOP* is a way to pause and give ourselves an opportunity to make a different decision (Linehan 2015). STOP is an acronym that reminds us to focus on slowing down so that we can make more mindful choices.

**S** = stop

**T** = take a step back

**O** = observe what is happening to you and also others

**P** = proceed mindfully (and with lots of self-compassion)

You can use the STOP skill in just a minute or two or, if urges to engage in self-damaging behaviors are particularly strong, you can decide how this skill might look over an hour, two hours, or even a day. The longer you can use this skill, the more likely you are to make a mindful, self-compassionate decision that won't hurt you or others.

Because of the very nature of impulsive behaviors, using a skill like STOP can be very challenging when you have an urge to react quickly on a thought or an emotion. As with all the skills, the more you use them, the easier they become.

You can remember to use a skill like STOP by planning on asking yourself, "Would I benefit from using STOP right now?" several times a day. You could set a reminder notification on your phone to do a quick check-in. The more you ask yourself about using STOP, the easier it will be to use it when you really need it.

# How to Use This Skill

You can use the STOP skill any time you want to slow things down long enough to make a wise, effective, and healthy decision.

Some people may be able to work through all the parts of STOP in just a few minutes, but others may need to use this skill over a longer period of time—like several hours or even a day. You don't have to be in a rush to use this skill. There's nothing wrong with taking each part of STOP and using it for ten or fifteen minutes. You might find that the longer you can stretch this skill out, the better. The following worksheet will help you get the most out of using STOP. The worksheet can also be found at http://www.newharbinger.com/55664.

## Practicing STOP

What do you think about using a skill like STOP to help you make choices that you won't regret later?

Can you think of any potential downsides of using the STOP skill?

_____

_____

_____

Using sticky notes or other reminders (like a bracelet or a wristband) can be a way to keep the skills in front of you when you are first learning and using them. What could help you remember to use the STOP skill— even if it's for just five or ten minutes?

_____

_____

Self-compassionate people usually aren't rushing through DBT skills; rather, they act with a lot of careful intention. What might help you remember to take your time using this skill?

_____

_____

_____

Sometimes it's nice to act with a lot of spontaneity. It can relieve boredom, it may be a part of your values, or it could be something that is part of your life worth living. Is there a way for you to simultaneously use the STOP skill and still make self-compassionate, responsible choices?

_____

_____

_____

## • *Kaci's Story*

*Kaci was no stranger to impulsive, self-sabotaging behaviors, and these behaviors often caused a lot of additional stress in her life.*

*Since she was sixteen years old, Kaci has worked as both a host and a server at several restaurants in her small town, but there were problems that seemed to come up again and again. Kaci was a hard worker who was willing to come to work early, stay late, and even cover extra shifts for her coworkers. However, she didn't always like how the restaurant was managed or she didn't approve of the shifts she was given to work, so she would sometimes complain to her coworkers and, on a few occasions, would tell regular diners how she thought the restaurant could be managed better. After a few months of working at a new restaurant, Kaci was either no longer added to the schedule or would be told that they had enough help for that week and that she wouldn't be needed.*

*Soon thereafter, Kaci would get hired at another restaurant and similar problems would come up again.*

*Kaci also found that she had a lot of difficulty getting along with her roommates. If they were too loud or too messy, Kaci would start to argue and even threatened legal action if the offending roommate didn't follow her house rules and expectations. After one particularly heated argument with a roommate that left that individual feeling physically threatened by Kaci's reaction, Kaci told her therapist, "I don't let anyone disrespect me. If I threatened anyone—and I don't think I did— they deserved it."*

*Kaci's therapist talked to her about how reacting before she gave herself the room she needed to think about the consequences of her behavior might be hurting her more than she imagined. She went on to explain that using a skill like STOP might even help Kaci be more self-compassionate. Kaci admitted, "It's true that I'm hard on others, but I'm also hard on myself." She also said that her anger would come up in a way that she felt immediately compelled to act on the emotion—even though it meant that she might experience a consequence she hadn't intended. When that would happen, she could get stuck in a cycle of repeating those same self-sabotaging behaviors.*

*Her therapist said, "Using the STOP skill can help you slow things down long enough so that you can make a self-compassionate decision that's in line with your goals." Together they talked about what it would look like to use STOP the next time she felt disrespected by a roommate or a boss and had an urge to complain or act in a way that others perceived as threatening.*

*As Kaci continued to work with the therapist, they identified more moments when she could weave both self-compassion and STOP into her day. Kaci found that when she used the STOP skill, she felt empowered and in control of her life. This is something that Kaci had rarely experienced before treatment. While all of her work and roommate problems weren't solved by being more self-compassionate or by using the STOP skill, Kaci felt like she had healthier ways of responding to those problems.*

Use the following worksheet to reflect on Kaci's story and how it is similar or different from your experience.

## Reflecting on Kaci's Story

Are there any elements of Kaci's story that resonate with you? How often are you acting without thinking about the consequences of your behavior?

_____

_____

_____

Imagine you are Kaci's best friend and she comes to you for advice because she is frustrated about her roommate, who doesn't clean the kitchen after she's done cooking dinner—preferring to wait until the next morning when she's less tired. What wisdom do you have for her when intense emotions come up and she has an urge to quickly act on them?

_____

_____

_____

When Kaci's therapist asked her to write a self-compassion script or narrative about how STOP might help her, she thought about how this skill gave her the emotional and physical space she needed to act in a different way. She wrote:

*I can be impulsive and self-sabotaging—especially when I'm angry. The STOP skill helps me slow things down so that I can remember what is most important to me.*

*The STOP skill allows me to respond to whatever is happening in the moment with more self-compassion and kindness. When I respond to my own frustration with compassion, I can be compassionate with others.*

What do you think of Kaci's self-compassion script? What would you want to remember when you think about reducing your own impulsive behaviors and replacing them with more self-compassionate moments?

_____

_____

_____

_____

_____

## • *Antoinette's Story*

*Antoinette was diagnosed with borderline personality disorder when she came to treatment shortly after she was arrested for shoplifting when she was nineteen years old. Making a twelve-month commitment to treatment was a part of her pretrial diversion program and she told her therapist that she was ready to make some permanent changes in her life. Antoinette told her therapist that she grew up in a home where many of her emotional and physical needs were often ignored or had gone unmet. Several years ago, shoplifting became something exciting for her to do after school with friends—instead of going home. The thrill and impulsive nature of stealing without being caught also helped her feel in control of a small part of her life.*

*When Antoinette's therapist explained how being more self-compassionate could help her heal from borderline personality disorder, Antoinette said, "Be compassionate toward myself after stealing for years? I got caught! That doesn't make sense." Antoinette's therapist explained, "Yes! Emotionally healthy people respond to their pain and suffering with more compassion and self-kindness. I want you to give yourself this important gift." Antoinette wasn't certain self-compassion would help, but she was willing to try.*

*Within a few months, Antoinette began to identify a few moments in her week when she could respond to her own pain with more compassion. Although she was doubtful that self-compassion could make a lasting difference, she found that it helped her feel just a little bit better. She also noticed that she had less of an urge to shoplift when she had an opportunity to do so.*

*Antoinette's therapist taught her several distress tolerance skills that she could use and her favorite was the STOP skill. She told her therapist, "I can always stop. I hadn't really understood that before. I thought that if I had an urge to do something that I had to follow through with that action. I don't have to act impulsively. I have other choices I can make."*

*As Antoinette's pretrial diversion program came to a close, Antoinette was proud of herself for meeting many of the goals she had created at the beginning of treatment. Life wasn't perfect but it was better, and Antoinette developed a plan for being more self-compassionate in the future.*

Use the following worksheet to reflect on Antoinette's story and how it is similar or different from your experience.

## Reflecting on Antoinette's Story

What elements of Antoinette's story resonate with you? Is her experience familiar to you?

_____

_____

_____

Using the STOP skill can be fairly difficult. What do you think are some of the drawbacks of pausing long enough to stop, take a step back, observe what's happening, and then proceed mindfully?

_____

_____

_____

_____

Remembering to use the STOP skill when you need it the most is a big challenge for most people who are learning the DBT skills. How could you remind yourself to practice this skill so that you're ready to use it when you need it?

_____

_____

_____

Antoinette's therapist also encouraged her to create a self-compassion script as part of her plan to help herself if urges to shoplift came up in the future. She wrote:

*I'm now able to understand the role of many impulsive and self-sabotaging behaviors in my life. I can respond to my past with a lot of self-compassion and remember that I have skills that I can use to help myself in the future.*

*STOP is one distress tolerance skill I can use to be a healthier me. I can slow down my actions and think about how to respond to my emotional needs in a more self-compassionate and less destructive way.*

What do you think about Antoinette's self-compassion script? Is there any other wisdom you have to share with Antoinette?

_____

_____

_____

_____

_____

_____

# Summary

- Impulsive behaviors are different than spontaneous behaviors.

- Self-destructive, illegal, or self-defeating behaviors that may make life more complicated are not a part of a life worth living.

- Understanding and acknowledging the consequences of impulsive behaviors can help you make wiser decisions.

- STOP (stop, take a step back, observe what's happening, and proceed mindfully) is a distress tolerance skill that helps you stay in control over what happens next in your day.

- Using a skill like STOP can give you time and space to make more self-compassionate, healthier decisions.

- You can remember to use the STOP skill with sticky notes or other reminders (like a bracelet or a wristband) when you are first learning and using it.

Add your own ideas below.

- _____

- _____

# CHAPTER 6

# Suicidal Thinking and Self-Harming Actions

Many people with borderline personality disorder think about harming themselves or they may even have urges to end their lives. Complete the following worksheet to assess how prevalent this symptom is for you. This worksheet can also be found at http://www.newharbinger.com/55664.

## Assessing Suicidal Thinking and Self-Harming Behaviors

Has this symptom of borderline personality disorder been problematic for you?

_____

_____

How has suicidal thinking or self-harming behaviors made your life more challenging?

_____

_____

_____

Have you ever thought about how a self-compassion practice might help decrease suicidal thoughts or self-harming behaviors? If so, how might greater self-compassion help you?

_____

_____

If thinking about suicide or engaging in self-harm are part of your life, I'd love for you to think about the benefits of sharing these emotions, thoughts, and urges with others. My hope is that you can share this important—and vulnerable—part of your story with someone like:

- A nonjudgmental friend
- An encouraging family member
- A social worker or case manager
- Your psychiatrist or nurse practitioner
- A validating therapist
- A peer support provider
- A support or 12-step group
- A sobriety coach

Please take a moment to list three people in your life who are ready to listen to you when you need it the most.

1. _____

2. _____

3. _____

You may also benefit from having other resources ready. People want to help, but you'll need to be brave and courageous enough to reach out for help.

**Suicide Prevention Lifeline**
988lifeline.org
Call or text 988

**Warm Lines**
warmline.org
These are often local peer-run organizations. Help may not be available 24/7.

**7 Cups**
7cups.com
This is an international organization of trained volunteer listeners available to chat, text, or talk.

**Veterans Crisis Line**

veteranscrisisline.net

Call or text 988 and press 1

**National Alliance on Mental Illness (NAMI) Help Line**

nami.org/support-education/nami-helpline

Text 62640

If you are outside the United States, please go to unsuicide.org for a comprehensive list of helpful organizations throughout the world. You'll also find additional resources in the back of this book.

For my clients who want to learn more about self-harming behaviors, I recommend *Freedom from Self-Harm: Overcoming Self-Injury with Skills from DBT and Other Treatments* by Kim L. Gratz and Alexander L. Chapman (New Harbinger Publications, 2009).

# Your Life Is Worth Living

In the early 1980s, when DBT creator Marsha Linehan was studying suicide prevention, she developed a tool called the Reasons for Living Scale to help people identify and understand their reasons for staying alive. You can find this tool with a quick online search or you can ask a mental health professional about using this assessment in treatment.

Do you have reasons for living today? If so, what are they? Check off some of your reasons for living and come up with some additional reasons for choosing self-compassion and commit to living.

☐ Sometimes life isn't so bad.

☐ I have friends who love me.

☐ I have a lot of hope that life will be easier when I'm consistently self-compassionate.

☐ Life is challenging but I'm up for the challenge.

☐ I want to help others who are suffering.

☐ I have a lot of plans I'm working on right now.

☐ I have good problem-solving skills.

☐ I am a hopeful person.

☐ Other people are ready to help me get the help I need.

☐ I want to write a book.

☐ I have a special event that I want to attend.

☐ I think that staying alive is a sign of wisdom.

☐ I can channel my emotional suffering into art, dance, music, or writing.

☐ I am learning to like myself just the way I am.

☐ Things are getting just a little bit better.

☐ I have ideas for making the world a kinder place.

☐ I am inherently worthy of healing and recovery.

☐ I can survive borderline personality disorder.

☐ My diagnosis does not dictate my actions.

☐ I can find meaning in my pain.

☐ I believe in myself.

☐ I want to stay alive to see what life will be like in the year 2050.

☐ I value life even when life is tough.

☐ Family members would be sad if I died.

☐ My dog, cat, bunny, or hamster would miss me.

☐ I am someone who overcomes difficulties.

☐ I can love myself through difficult times in life.

☐ I am a resilient person.

☐ Other: _____

☐ Other: _____

☐ Other: _____

You don't need twenty or a hundred reasons for living. Identifying and reminding yourself of just one or two ideas each day may help you resist urges to think about or plan suicide.

Next, I'd love for you to tell someone else about your reason for living. Could you reach out today and share your ideas with a family member, friend, social worker, 12-step sponsor, or therapist? You could also ask the important people in your life about their reasons for staying alive. In my opinion, the more ideas you have, the better.

# Self-Compassion Skill: Self-Soothing as a Self-Compassionate Behavior

Using the DBT distress tolerance skill of *self-soothing* with your five senses is the opposite of self-harm. Self-soothing with your five senses is a beautiful way to care for yourself when emotions are running high and urges to self-harm are present. A step toward self-compassion means that you don't engage in any behaviors where you would temporarily or permanently harm yourself.

*Note:* Self-soothing is not meant to be a way to avoid real world responsibilities, work, or other "adulting" activities. You don't want to get lost in self-soothing so that it becomes a mindless activity—like scrolling on your phone for an hour.

Before you use this self-compassion skill, ask yourself:

- Am I using this idea for a short period of time (thirty minutes or less) to help myself?

or

- Am I using self-soothing to escape or avoid problems?

The following worksheet will help you identify different ways to self-soothe with your five senses. Generate as many ideas as possible. This worksheet can also be found at http://www.newharbinger.com/55664.

## Self-Soothing with My Five Senses

**Sight:** Can you think of ways to self-soothe with the sense of sight? For instance, could you go to a nice park and spend twenty minutes looking for wildflowers? Could you look through the pages of a favorite art or photography book?

List the ways you can self-soothe with sight or vision in the space below:

_____

_____

_____

_____

**Smell:** How many ways can you self-soothe with scent or smell? Could you bake cookies or bread just for the yummy scent? What about lighting a lavender-scented candle? Does the scent of freshly mown grass make you happy? What about the scent of rain?

List the ways you can self-soothe with scent or smell in the space below:

_____

_____

_____

_____

**Touch:** How often do you self-soothe with touch? Many people find it soothing to wrap themselves up in a favorite blanket or quilt. Do you ever cuddle with a stuffed animal or a special doll you've had since childhood? Petting your cat or dog can be a way for you to self-soothe with touch. Maybe you also have a pair of warm socks that helps you feel more relaxed when you put them on your feet.

List the ways you can self-soothe with touch in the space below:

_____

_____

_____

_____

**Taste:** Taste is another way to soothe yourself. A small piece of chocolate or candy can be a way to self-soothe for a few minutes at a time. When it comes to this way of self-soothing, pay close attention to mindless eating and remember that less is more. Don't give in to the urge of telling yourself that eating an entire pint of ice cream is self-soothing.

List the ways you can self-soothe with taste in the space below:

_____

_____

_____

_____

**Sound:** Do you ever self-soothe with sound or hearing? Do you have what I call a "Happy Music Playlist" of songs or music that increases your happiness or makes you feel like dancing? Lots of people like to relax to nature sounds or birdsongs. Sometimes sitting in silence for just five minutes can be soothing for many people.

List the ways you can self-soothe with sound in the space below:

_____

_____

_____

_____

Now you are armed with a lot of good ideas. Feel free to continue to come back to this section of the book and continue to add more ideas as you collect them.

## How to Use This Skill

You can increase the likelihood of your success in using the self-soothing skills by prioritizing this skill set each day.

Create a seven-day, ten-day, or thirty-day plan to use at least two self-soothing skills every day. It may seem like a lot of work, but I've seen its effectiveness so many times. I really believe in it! Your commitment to self-soothing may make that much of a difference in your life.

By creating this plan, you are communicating to yourself and others, "I am worthy of self-kindness," or "It's okay for me to be self-compassionate by _____." Self-soothing really is that important for individuals with a diagnosis of borderline personality disorder.

The following worksheet will help you explore self-soothing activities. This worksheet can also be found at http://www.newharbinger.com/55664.

## My Self-Soothing Activities

If you had to pick one self-soothing skill to use between now and the time you go to bed tonight, what would it be?

_____

Daily self-soothing isn't always convenient or easy to practice. Do you have any ideas about how to fit this skill into your life? What might help?

_____

_____

_____

What else might help you prioritize self-soothing as an act of self-compassion several times a day?

_____

_____

Mutual accountability with a friend or family member may be helpful. Do you have someone in your life who would be willing to practice these skills with you? Write down their names below along with any ideas for how you could use these self-soothing skills together.

_____

_____

_____

_____

## • *Hope's Story*

*Hope was twenty-one years old when she first met with a DBT therapist. She had dropped out of college and had stopped working at her family's business. Hope explained to the therapist, "My name is ironic because I often feel hopeless. I feel like a failure at whatever I do and I don't see a future for myself." When asked about a history of self-harming behaviors, Hope said, "Yes, I sometimes hurt myself. It helps me feel better for a few minutes at a time, but afterward I'm back to hating myself. This isn't the way I want to live. I need help, but it feels like I'm in too deep. It's like I'm drowning in my own sadness. I can't find the life raft." When asked about how self-compassionate she was, Hope said, "My mom always says that I'm my worst enemy. I guess that's true."*

*Hope's therapist also talked to her about her reasons for staying alive and what it might look like to make a serious commitment to an evidence-based treatment like DBT that would probably be difficult at times.*

*First, Hope was able to identify several reasons for staying alive. They included:*

- *Hope was just sixteen credits shy of an undergraduate degree in social work. She longed to return to school to complete her degree.*

- *In spite of feeling hopeless a lot of the time, she believed in her ability to help others who were hurting. She said that helping others also helped her.*

- *Finally, Hope grew up on a ranch and talked about how much she loved riding and caring for her two horses. Her horses needed her and taking care of the animals on the family's ranch was another reason for her to stay alive.*

*After a few sessions with the therapist, and a conversation weighing the pros and cons of treatment with several family members, Hope said that she wanted to make a commitment to learning and practicing the DBT skills. That commitment to treatment meant that Hope would be willing to use skills to help herself when she felt like harming herself.*

*Over the next several months, Hope started to learn skills that would help her manage her thoughts, emotions, and urges to engage in self-harming behaviors. At one point, Hope's therapist encouraged her to come up with a list of a hundred ways that she could soothe herself when urges to self-harm were particularly strong. Hope took the homework assignment seriously and showed up at her next appointment ready with a hundred ideas for self-soothing with her five senses that she could use to help herself. Hope even took the assignment to the next level and categorized her ideas like this:*

- *Ideas for self-soothing at home*

- *Ideas for self-soothing in the car*

- *Ideas for self-soothing in the classroom*

- *Ideas for self-soothing on sad days*

- *Ideas for self-soothing when I feel afraid*

- *Ideas for self-soothing when I feel like arguing*

*Hope and her therapist talked about how Hope could begin to use these ideas the next time she thought about harming herself. Her therapist said, "Self-soothing is an act of self-compassion. The more you practice, the easier it will be to resist the urges. You can do this and I believe in you."*

*After twelve months of treatment, Hope observed, "In the beginning, I was dismissive of the idea of self-soothing as a skill, but it works. If I can identify the urge, I can take the next step and do something kind for myself. I didn't know how to self-soothe, but now I do. It's one of my favorite tools to use. It's part of the life raft that keeps me afloat when I feel really sad."*

Use the following worksheet to reflect on Hope's story and how it is similar or different from your experience.

## Reflecting on Hope's Story

What are the parts of Hope's story that resonate with you?

_____

_____

_____

In the past, how have you coped with urges to engage in self-harming behaviors?

_____

_____

_____

_____

What do you think about Hope's idea for coming up with ideas for self-soothing in different places or when different emotions come up for her? Could you do something similar?

_____

_____

_____

When Hope's therapist asked her to write a self-compassion script or narrative about how self-soothing with her five senses might help her, she wanted to remind herself that this was a healthy way of coping with unwanted thoughts and emotions. She wrote:

> *DBT is helping me learn that I can be self-compassionate when I think about hurting myself.*
>
> *The skill of self-soothing reminds me that I am worthy of loving myself like I love others. This is a skill I can use for the rest of my life to cope with problems in a healthier way.*

Using an online graphic design tool, Hope created a little 5 x 7 poster that read, "Self-soothing is an act of self-compassion." She had the poster printed and framed. Hope hung it above her nightstand so that she could remind herself that giving herself permission to self-soothe was a healthy, responsible choice she could make each day.

What do you think of Hope's self-compassion script? What would you want to remember about responding to urges to engage in self-harming behaviors or think about suicide?

Create your own self-compassion script about using self-soothing skills as a way to cope with self-harm urges or suicidal thinking in the space below.

_____

_____

_____

_____

_____

## • *Jackson's Story*

*Jackson was recommended to a DBT therapist shortly after a serious suicide attempt that had put him in the hospital for almost a week.*

*During his initial assessment, his therapist talked to Jackson about his reasons for staying alive and not dying by suicide. Jackson talked a lot about self-hatred and how difficult it was for him to picture a future where life was meaningful. As a part of his assessment, his therapist gave him a copy of Marsha Linehan's Reasons for Living Scale.*

*After reviewing the list of ideas and talking through them during a session, Jackson identified a few reasons for staying alive. They included:*

- *I want to know how my college football team will do next year.*

- *I think that suicide creates problems for the people left behind.*

- *I want to go back to Colorado to hike in the summer.*

*Together Jackson and his therapist continued to talk about his big reasons to stay alive and some very small reasons to live. His therapist wanted to hear more about Jackson's love for hiking and camping. He talked about how he loved to be in nature. His therapist asked, "Tell me more about what being in nature does for you and your emotional health." He answered by saying, "Last September I went backpacking in Colorado with some friends and I remember feeling really alive. I wasn't worried. I wasn't depressed. I felt connected to the land, the birds, and the mountains. I was still me, but I was a better me that week." Jackson's therapist wondered out loud whether future hiking trips could be a part of what Marsha Linehan calls "a life worth living." Jackson mentioned that another trip was being planned this coming spring and that he thought he could join his friends.*

*As he began to learn a lot of DBT skills that would help him create the life he really desired, Jackson began to think of other ways to get in touch with nature and being outdoors. For many years, Jackson had worked in software development through short-term freelance contracts but often found the work too tedious and, in his words, "boring and depressing." He had read about fire lookout jobs in Oregon and Washington and that sounded appealing to him. He reasoned that he might be able to balance this kind of work six months out of the year while working his regular job the other six months. Even if he couldn't find employment as a fire observer, he was open to other work that would allow him to be in nature most of the time.*

*Jackson's therapist helped him think of other ways that he could use the DBT skill of self-soothing outdoors. For instance, what could he do to self-soothe with all his five senses while hiking or camping? For homework that week, Jackson was asked to make a list of all of the ways he could be compassionate with himself by engaging in regular self-soothing. While thinking about the assignment on his way home from therapy, Jackson remembered hearing about a local kayaking organization that went out for a group paddle twice a month. He would add that opportunity to his list knowing he would find that to be a relaxing activity.*

*The next week when Jackson and his therapist met, she said, "You've come up with a lot of great ideas for self-soothing while you're outdoors. I'd love for you to start implementing some of them this week. Are you willing to do that?" Jackson said that he was up for the challenge.*

Use the following worksheet to reflect on Jackson's story and how it is similar or different from your experience.

## Reflecting on Jackson's Story

What elements of Jackson's story resonate with you? Is his experience familiar to you?

_____

_____

_____

Jackson helped generate ideas for self-soothing when he told his therapist about an enjoyable trip to Colorado with his friends. List past experiences that could help you find ways to self-soothe in the future?

_____

_____

_____

What other wisdom would you want to share with Jackson about how practicing self-soothing could increase his capacity for self-compassion?

_____

_____

_____

_____

Jackson's therapist also encouraged him to create a self-compassion script as part of his plan to help himself when a sad day or a depressive mood came up. He wrote:

*I'm at my best when I'm outdoors and in nature. I don't hate myself when I'm hiking. Instead of telling myself that I don't have the time or am too tired, I can prioritize self-soothing as a way to affirm my choice to stay alive.*

*For me, self-soothing by being outdoors is a way for me to practice self-compassion. It's the opposite of self-hatred.*

What do you think about Jackson's observation that self-compassion is the opposite of self-hatred? Could that be true for you?

_____

_____

_____

_____

_____

The following worksheet will help you integrate self-soothing into your daily routine. This worksheet can also be found at http://www.newharbinger.com/55664.

# My Self-Soothing Plan

What would a full day of self-soothing look like for you? Complete the schedule below and list all the ways you could use these ideas throughout your day.

6:00 a.m. _____

7:00 a.m. _____

8:00 a.m. _____

9:00 a.m. _____

10:00 a.m. _____

11:00 a.m. _____

12:00 p.m. _____

1:00 p.m. _____

2:00 p.m. _____

3:00 p.m. _____

4:00 p.m. _____

5:00 p.m. _____

6:00 p.m. _____

7:00 p.m. _____

8:00 p.m. _____

9:00 p.m. _____

10:00 p.m. _____

11:00 p.m. _____

How might your future be different if you prioritized self-soothing most days of the week? Think about how this practice might improve your relationships with those closest to you.

_____

_____

_____

## Summary

- Self-soothing is another distress tolerance skill.

- You can self-soothe with any of your five senses.

- Making a list of different ways to self-soothe in advance of needing the skills will help you stay ready when you need to implement these ideas.

- Self-soothing is the opposite of self-hatred.

- Emotionally healthy people often prioritize self-soothing. Self-soothing is a way you can practice self-compassion.

- Regular self-soothing may be an important part of your life worth living.

Add your own ideas below.

- _____

- _____

# CHAPTER 7

# Intense and Ever-Changing Emotions

Do you have a lot of big emotions that sometimes create more trouble for you?

For a lot of people, problematic or unwanted emotions seem to create more problematic emotions, and the cycle of emotions and emotional reactions can be challenging to stop once it starts. Many people with borderline personality disorder have observed that it feels like they are living from one big emotional experience to another without a lot of breathing room in between. Because those ever-changing and overwhelming emotions can interfere in your relationships, with work life, and with goals that are important to you, it can be a pretty exhausting and difficult way to live. Complete the following worksheet to assess how prevalent this symptom is for you. This worksheet can also be found at http://www.newharbinger.com/55664.

## Assessing Your Emotional Life

Has this symptom of rapidly changing or strong emotions ever been problematic for you?

_____

_____

_____

_____

How have your emotional responses and reactions negatively interfered with your relationships, work, education, or reaching other goals that are important to you?

_____

_____

_____

_____

How often are you able to respond to strong emotional reactions with self-compassion?

_____

_____

_____

_____

Of course, not all emotions or emotional experiences are problematic or exhausting. There is plenty to love about positive emotions. To help demonstrate this idea, check off the emotions that you want to cultivate more of in your life.

☐ happy                      ☐ enthusiastic

☐ joyful                     ☐ compassionate

☐ content                    ☐ hopeful

☐ peaceful                   ☐ satisfied

☐ confident                  ☐ surprised

☐ loved                      ☐ delighted

☐ thankful                   ☐ proud

If you have other enjoyable or positive emotions you have mindfully observed and want to cultivate in your life, list those below:

_____

_____

_____

Many people with borderline personality disorder spend a lot of time and energy thinking about and feeling their unwanted or undesired emotions. It can be difficult to let go of or disengage from the unwanted emotions. These emotions may include sadness, loneliness, anger, shame, guilt, embarrassment, or hopelessness.

In her skills training manual, Marsha Linehan (2015) writes that emotions are neither good nor bad, but your judgments about your emotions can keep the cycle of emotional reactivity going longer than necessary. You won't be surprised to learn that being more self-compassionate can reduce the intensity and duration of a difficult emotional experience.

Here are a few examples of how this could work:

*Jacob had a problem with road rage and found that his anger could often climb pretty quickly when he was on his way to work and was stuck in slow-moving traffic. It seemed like once he got angry, he got angrier and would arrive at work in a bad mood on most days.*

When Jacob began to name his anger out loud, he found that it usually helped him stay in control. If he could say to himself, "A lot of people feel anger when they are driving, so, in that way, I'm not really any different than anyone else on the road," Jacob found that his anger was more manageable. While he was still frustrated a lot of the time, Jacob's self-compassion practice around his emotional experience helped him better manage his mood most days.

*As a child, Janey experienced a lot of shyness when she was in school. When she became an adult and started college, her shyness evolved into what looked like social anxiety. She would feel fairly confident when she was at home or with people she knew, but if she was around a lot of strangers, her anxiety would begin to climb.*

After working with a DBT therapist, Janey began to put words to her emotional experience. To help reduce her anxiety, she would self-compassionately describe to herself, "I'm experiencing anxiety right now. I don't know anyone in this class, so it makes sense that I'm feeling pretty awkward in this moment." She found that naming her emotions and using some compassionate self-talk made it possible for her to stay in the classroom when she felt like leaving.

# Self-Compassion Skill: Loving Your Emotions with Mindfulness

Now we'll look at how a self-compassion practice of loving your emotions may help you stay in control or regain control of your emotional experiences and emotional expressions. These ideas aren't meant to convince you that your emotions aren't real or valid but to help you imagine that self-compassion can be an important tool to assist you in managing your emotions so you can stay true to your values and goals. You can balance validating your emotions and, simultaneously, loving your emotions.

What does it mean to "love" your emotions?

In her skills training book, Marsha Linehan (2015) writes about the DBT skill of mindfulness of emotions and says that one way to practice this skill is to *love all of your emotions*. Marsha Linehan doesn't mean that you should "like" your emotions, nor does she believe that you should just accept the emotions you already love. She's serious; she wants you to think about the benefits of loving all of your emotions. That includes the difficult emotions you may experience each day.

Think about the potential advantages of loving your emotions. This means that, as a way of skillfully coping with unwanted emotions, you might decide to respond to difficult emotions with love and acceptance. It's a radical idea to implement—especially when you want to run or hide from your emotions. For instance, you could ask yourself:

- Could I benefit from loving myself throughout a depressive episode or as I grieve?

- Is it possible to love myself when I feel frustrated or annoyed?

- Could I love feelings of shame or guilt for what they are or what they can teach me on a difficult day?

- Is there something for me to learn from this emotional experience?

- How could I respond to this emotional pain self-compassionately and lovingly?

Responding to difficult emotions with love for those emotions is a profound and life-changing act of self-compassion. Here are some of the potential benefits you might experience when you approach your emotions with love:

- Responding to your emotions with love is a nonjudgmental, self-kind act.

- Emotional self-hatred doesn't help you grow or be your best self.

- Emotions help you communicate with others.

- There may be something that you can learn about yourself from your emotion reactions.

- Emotions can help validate your experiences or help you find your own wisdom.

- Your emotions can point you toward understanding more about your values.

- Emotions are a normal part of being alive.

- Your emotional sensitivity may be a gift that helps others.

- Emotions are evidence of being a healthy human experiencing normal reactions.

Can you think of any other benefits? List them below.

_____

_____

## How to Use This Skill

You can use the skill of mindfulness of emotions by allowing yourself to be open and curious about your emotions and emotional experiences. For example, you might experience some pretty intense anger and then think to yourself, "Wow. I got really upset over that. Maybe it was more important to me than I first imagined. I wonder why I reacted so strongly." Or you could tell yourself on a sad day, "Staying at home isn't going to help me feel better. How can I be kind to myself when I'm struggling so much today?"

Mindfulness of emotions isn't about denying your emotions or pushing them away. It's not about avoiding painful emotional experiences. The following worksheet will help you explore how to use this skill with self-compassion. This worksheet can also be found at http://www.newharbinger.com/55664.

## Exploring Mindfulness of Emotions

Being mindful of emotions is a skill that can be uncomfortable to use. What gets in the way of loving your emotions or your emotional experiences?

_____

_____

_____

_____

What advice would you give someone who says, "Love my emotions?? That's not going to help me!"?

_____

_____

_____

## • *Ryan's Story*

*Ryan was diagnosed with borderline personality disorder after a physical altercation with his best friend that ended their friendship of almost twenty years.*

*When Ryan first met with a DBT therapist, he stated that one of his goals was to find better friends and get up the courage to permanently leave the town where he grew up. Ryan stated that he had few friends and felt like he couldn't trust others. He said that his expression of anger often scared others and getting into a fight with his best friend was "the last straw" for him. His therapist wanted to hear more about his anger, so Ryan explained, "I just can't control myself sometimes. I feel disrespected or I think I'm being disrespected and I lose control. I don't know why that happens, but I can't keep doing this. At some point I'm going to get arrested or worse."*

*When asked about how self-compassionate he was when anger came up, Ryan replied, "I'm not. Why would I be nice to myself when I'm angry?" Ryan's therapist explained that being kind to himself when feelings of anger came up might help him so that he doesn't ever respond with violence again.*

*Ryan's therapist asked, "When are you more likely to stay in control: when you are hating yourself or others or when you are being kind to yourself? That's the benefit of self-compassion. This anger is coming from somewhere. The more you can name it and understand it, the less problematic it will be. In that way, loving your emotion is a very practical way you can help yourself."*

*No one had ever made this suggestion to Ryan. Instead, people told him to "stop being so angry," "control yourself," or "pull it together." When Ryan couldn't control his anger, he felt a lot of shame and that led to more anger toward himself and others. That painful cycle contributed to the ending of an important friendship.*

*As Ryan and his therapist continued to work together, Ryan began to practice the DBT skill of mindfulness of emotions. He noticed that when he could name the emotion, he could take the next step and be kind to himself as he experienced that emotion. He admitted that he couldn't love his emotions yet, but he was getting closer to acceptance.*

*A year later, Ryan reflected that this one self-compassion practice helped him learn more about his emotions and why he felt the way he did. Loving his emotions wasn't easy, but he consistently saw the benefits of responding to his emotions with self-compassion and curiosity. On the anniversary of his first session, he told his therapist, "I still get angry. Why shouldn't I? It's a normal emotion that everyone has. The difference is now I can manage it. These are skills I needed when I was growing up but didn't have. Telling myself not to be angry just made me angrier."*

Use the following worksheet to reflect on Ryan's story and how it is similar or different from your experience.

## Reflecting on Ryan's Story

How have you coped with emotions that you didn't love? Think about how you've responded to your own feelings of sadness, anger, shame, guilt, or embarrassment.

_____

_____

_____

_____

Ryan didn't grow up knowing how to respond to his anger. Why do you think that learning how to love all of his emotions made such a difference for him as an adult?

_____

_____

_____

The idea of loving your emotions does not come easily or naturally for most people who have a diagnosis of borderline personality disorder. If you had judgments about this skill idea, what do you think after reading Ryan's story?

_____

_____

_____

As a part of their work together, Ryan's therapist asked him to create a self-compassion script that he could read to himself when he felt angry in the future. Here's what he wrote:

*I can hurt others when anger comes up in my life or I can respond to my emotions with self-compassion. Loving myself in my anger is healthier than hating myself in my anger. My anger gives me a lot of information about what is important to me. If I didn't care, I wouldn't get angry.*

*I can make the choice to love my emotions.*

What do you think about Ryan's script? Create a similar script to read to yourself when difficult or challenging emotions come up for you.

_____

_____

_____

_____

## • *Kait's Story*

*Kait is twenty-two years old and the manager of a vintage book and gaming store. She has been diagnosed with borderline personality disorder and also has recurring major depressive episodes.*

*Over many years and with lots of excellent treatment, Kait learned how to manage many of her symptoms. She loved her work, but when episodes of deep sadness came up in her life, it was tempting to miss work and think about quitting. While she had an excellent relationship with the store's owner, Kait valued being someone who was dependable and worked when she was scheduled to work. She could ask for time off when she needed it, but she also admitted that she often felt better when she "forced" herself to go to work. Kait's therapist asked her, "That doesn't necessarily sound like self-compassion. How do you find a balance between forcing yourself to do something that might, indeed, help, and choosing self-compassion when you are experiencing a depressive episode?"*

*Kait admitted that she was still trying to understand that part of her healing and recovery from depression. She said, "This may be something that I have to deal with for the rest of my life. I want to work and I might also need to take some extra days off for some additional self-care. I know that usually helps me get through the worst of a depressive episode." Then Kait's therapist asked, "What would it look like for you to love yourself through the sadness that you sometimes still experience? Can you love the emotion? Could you find a way to love the sadness?"*

Kait had never thought of it that way. Her depression was almost always accompanied by a lot of guilt and sometimes shame over missing work, and then she experienced even more sadness and depression. It had been a painful emotional cycle for Kait. Loving sadness or her depression felt like it wouldn't work, but Kait had to admit that the excessive guilt and self-hatred over taking time off wasn't helping her feel better any faster.

Together with her therapist, Kait began to use the DBT skill of mindfulness of emotions for loving her sadness during a depressive episode. Instead of diving into the deep end of guilt and feeling worse, Kait was willing to do something completely different.

Part of the plan they created to use this skill looked like this:

**Step 1:** Name the emotion (like sadness, guilt, or hopelessness) and commit to physical safety for the duration of the depressive episode.

**Step 2:** Reach out to the store owner about taking a day or two off.

**Step 3:** Practice loving the emotion of sadness, especially when unjustified guilt or shame comes up.

**Step 4:** Engage in other self-compassionate acts and gestures. For instance, shower, get dressed in clean clothes, and leave the house for at least twenty minutes once a day.

**Step 5:** Stay in touch with the store owner about returning to work. Return texts or calls within eight hours. Don't hide! Don't ghost!

**Step 6:** Weigh the pros and cons of "forcing" a return to work before being ready.

**Step 7:** Use a DBT diary card or app to keep track of emotions, urges, and behaviors.

**Step 8:** Stay in touch with friends and ask for extra help when needed.

Kait felt a little overwhelmed with the plan but imagined that she could probably work with it. She kept a paper copy of her plan in her backpack, but she also had a copy on her phone. When she needed to use her plan, she'd be ready.

Almost two months later, Kait felt a depressive episode coming on and quickly committed to following the plan she had developed with her therapist. She reached out to her therapist for some additional accountability and said, "I'm going to try loving myself through this episode."

Use the following worksheet to reflect on Kait's story and how it is similar or different from your experience.

# Reflecting on Kait's Story

What elements of Kait's story resonate with you? Is her experience familiar to you?

_____

_____

_____

What obstacles or judgments have come up for you when you've thought about loving your emotions?

_____

_____

_____

In this story, Kait made a choice about "loving herself" though a depressive episode. Why do you think this commitment helped her help herself?

_____

_____

_____

During their next session, Kait's therapist also encouraged her to create a self-compassion script to help remind herself about loving the emotions she was experiencing. As a homework assignment, Kait wrote:

_Excessive guilt and sadness keep me feeling depressed for longer periods of time. If I can love my emotions, I can reduce the intensity and length of a depressive episode._

_I want to remember that depression makes all of my emotions big and scary when they aren't. Mindfully loving my feelings as they come up makes them smaller and less scary. Following my plan and being self-compassionate is a healthier response to my depression._

If you created a similar self-compassion script for a strong, recurring emotion, what would you include?

_____

_____

_____

_____

_____

Remember that emotions are a normal and healthy part of the human experience. Our emotions give us a lot of important information about who we are and what we value. They also give us additional data about our personal goals and hopes for the future.

Emotions also help us communicate with others, and we can use our emotions to help understand ourselves. While some emotions can be stronger or felt more intensely than others, they are still a normal part of being a human in a suffering world.

Could this wisdom help you be more accepting of difficult emotional experiences? Can this idea give you the permission and room you need to love your more challenging emotions? Please feel free to explore this idea in the space below.

_____

_____

_____

_____

_____

_____

_____

_____

# Summary

- Your emotions are part of who you are but they do not define who you are.

- Emotions can give you a lot of information about who you are and what you value. Your emotions also help you communicate with others.

- Loving your emotions is an important step on the journey toward self-compassion.

- The DBT skill of mindfulness of emotions can help you understand and manage unwanted emotions.

- Self-compassionate individuals are more likely to tolerate difficult emotions when they come up.

- Your emotional wellness comes down to the small, consistent choices you make each day to improve your life.

Add your own ideas below.

- _____

- _____

# CHAPTER 8

# Chronic Feelings of Emptiness and Boredom

One of the things that comes up for a lot of people with a diagnosis of borderline personality disorder is the symptom of thinking, believing, or feeling that your life may not have purpose or meaning.

There are lots of different manifestations of this idea. On one hand, this might look like chronic boredom. You might be thinking that life in general—or more specifically, your life in this moment—is boring or meaningless. Sometimes people think, "I'm waiting for my life to get started," or "I'm waiting for (fill in the blank) to happen and then I won't feel bored. Life won't feel so empty." Complete the following worksheet to assess how prevalent this symptom is for you. This worksheet can also be found at http://www.newharbinger.com/55664.

## Assessing Feelings of Emptiness and Boredom

How often do you feel empty or bored? Have you ever thought, "I really just don't know that my life even matters"?

_____

_____

_____

How have feelings of emptiness or boredom kept you from pursuing goals that are important to you?

_____

_____

_____

How has emptiness or meaninglessness affected your relationships with others?

_____

_____

_____

There may be times during your day or week when life feels a little more boring or empty. For instance, if you are waiting for someone to return a call, text, or email, that might create some anxiety that can also look like boredom. This may also occur when you are waiting for something to happen. Perhaps you are waiting for a professor to grade an exam you studied hard for or you are expecting to hear back about a job you really want.

I believe that it's important to address this symptom of borderline personality disorder because it might affect how you see yourself or your relationships with others. Here's an example of how this might look for some people:

Rosa was diagnosed with borderline personality disorder when she was twenty-one years old and had just dropped out of college. When she learned about the diagnostic criterion of "feelings of emptiness," Rosa said to her therapist, "That's so me. I get excited about a class I registered for, but then after a few weeks, I'll usually lose interest. I don't understand it. I need the 'newness' or the excitement, and if I stop experiencing that, I drop it. I've done that so many times and it usually leads to some depression and even some suicidal thinking. I tell myself, 'You can't follow through and finish anything.' I don't like this part of myself."

That experience of meaninglessness can create depression for some individuals but, for others, they may experience this symptom with more anxiety or fear. Which is true for you?

_____

_____

_____

_____

_____

# Self-Compassion Skill: Helping Others Helps You

Have you ever heard of the concept of altruism? Altruism is defined as a selfless concern to act for others. This might look like helping a stranger change a flat tire while not expecting any money or other kind gesture in return. You may already know that when you help others, you also help yourself feel better, so not only can a random act of kindness be a way to show others compassion, but you may also create compassion for yourself.

There's a lot of scientific evidence to show that acting in a selfless way helps us feel better about ourselves. It can also be a way to create meaning and purpose for many people—leaving them feeling less empty. If this idea works for them, it might also work for you.

In DBT, we often talk about the distress tolerance skill of contributing (Linehan 2015). The idea behind the skill of contributing is pretty simple: Finding a way to contribute to others may help you manage unwanted thoughts and emotions.

You can get ready to practice this skill by generating a list of ten to twenty-five ideas for how you can contribute to others in a small way. It can be tempting to think that you need to do something big and important, but contributing may consist of a tiny act or gesture that may even be anonymous.

There are many ways to help others. Check off the ways you have helped others.

☐ I've bought a coworker coffee.

☐ I've stopped to help a stranger.

☐ I've sent friends texts, memes, or videos letting them know that I'm thinking about them.

☐ I've told a family member that I appreciate them.

☐ I've taken time out of my day to help a neighbor with a simple chore or errand.

☐ I've brought homemade baked goods to share with coworkers.

☐ I've written a "thank you" note to a professor or teacher.

☐ I've invited a friend to a holiday or birthday party.

☐ I've completed a household chore for a roommate or family member.

☐ I've sat quietly with a friend who was experiencing a loss.

☐ I've helped prepare a meal for a grandparent or older relative.

☐ I've smiled at a stranger at a store or on the street.

☐ I've helped a friend pack and move apartments.

☐ I've tutored or taught something to a classmate.

☐ I've held a door open for a stranger.

☐ I've picked up trash from a parking lot or on the side of the road.

☐ I've remembered friends on their birthdays.

☐ I've helped a friend find their lost pet.

☐ I've liked or shared a friend's social media post.

☐ I've surprised a work colleague with flowers on a difficult day.

☐ I've volunteered for a cause or organization that fits my values.

☐ I've let a friend borrow something valuable.

☐ I've donated to a nonprofit or religious organization that means a lot to me.

☐ I've been friendly to a customer service representative.

☐ I've visited someone in the hospital.

☐ I've offered to pick up a friend from the airport.

You may have other examples of how you have thoughtfully and selflessly helped family members, friends, and even strangers. Take a few moments and list them below.

- _____

- _____

- _____

- _____

- _____

Take another moment and write about how you felt after you completed some of these kind acts. If you feel comfortable, share your reflection with a friend, therapist, support group, or peer support provider. Keep in mind that others may be inspired when you share your examples just as you might be inspired by how others use the skill of contributing.

_____

_____

_____

_____

## How to Use This Skill

You can use this skill by thinking of ways you can contribute to others today. If you can, make a list of ideas that you can begin to implement over the next twenty-four hours. You don't want to wait too long to use this skill when you can benefit from contributing to others now.

If you are temporarily confined to your home and won't be interacting with others in person, you can think of ways to contribute to others by making a call, creating a short, funny video, or sending a text that says "I love you," "I'm thinking about you," or "I'm thankful that you're in my life."

The following worksheet will help you brainstorm ways to contribute. This worksheet can also be found at http://www.newharbinger.com/55664.

# Exploring Ways to Contribute

Sometimes people imagine that their kind gestures or acts won't make a difference for them or for others. Why do you think some people might believe that's true?

_____

_____

_____

Self-compassionate people are more likely to show compassion to others. Why do you think that might be so?

_____

_____

_____

Brainstorm ways, both big and small, that you can contribute to others.

_____

_____

_____

_____

_____

_____

_____

_____

_____

## • *Becca's Story*

*Becca was twenty-two years old when she first started treatment for borderline personality disorder and depression. She didn't know a lot about her BPD diagnosis but was willing to learn more. One of the things that helped her understand herself within the context of the diagnosis was to read stories about individuals who had recovered from BPD. In particular, her therapist recommended Beyond Borderline: True Stories of Recovery from Borderline Personality Disorder (New Harbinger, 2016) and Stronger Than BPD: The Girl's Guide to Taking Control of Intense Emotions, Drama, and Chaos Using DBT (New Harbinger, 2017).*

*Over the next couple of months, Becca read the books and discussed her impressions with her therapist during their weekly sessions. During this time of her life, Becca felt like she was having one "aha" moment after another. She told her therapist, "These symptoms have been a part of my life for a long time but I'm just now putting all the pieces together. I feel like I'm a one-woman, life-size jigsaw puzzle."*

*One of the things that kept coming up for her was the seventh diagnostic criterion of emptiness. Becca's therapist explained that emptiness could look like boredom on one end of the spectrum, and on the other end, it might look like an existential crisis—an inner conflict that sometimes left Becca wondering why she was ever born or thinking that life might always be difficult. Becca laughed and agreed. She said, "I've lived most of my life on that spectrum."*

*For homework that week, Becca's therapist challenged her to identify and journal about at least three meaningful moments over the next seven days. She explained that they didn't need to be anything that felt too big and imagined that Becca might find meaning or purpose in something small.*

*Becca came back the next week with a story she was looking forward to sharing. She said that she had been at the library the past week. She was behind a woman who was checking out some books when she overheard the librarian tell her that she had an overdue book fine of sixty-five cents. The stranger started to go through her bag to find some change to pay the fine when Becca uncharacteristically spoke up and asked, "I've got a dollar. May I please give it to you?" The woman graciously agreed and Becca said that she felt amazing for the remainder of the day. She told her therapist, "This was a meaningful moment for me! It was so small, but it felt important. Doing something for someone else helped me feel better that day."*

*Becca's therapist tied this observation to the self-compassion work they had been doing over the previous month and said, "It sounds like you used the DBT skill of contributing to others. You helped yourself by helping others. Not only was this a compassionate gesture toward a stranger but we could also call it self-compassionate. You are treating others like how you want to be treated. Congratulations!"*

*Later that evening, Becca spent some time reflecting on the idea of how helping others could be a way to show compassion toward herself. She thought about other times in her life when she stepped out of her comfort zone to help others and found that the outcome almost always meant that she liked herself a little more. Becca thought about how helping others was already a fit for her values. Maybe she could prioritize the skill of contributing as a part of her "life worth living" goal in treatment.*

Use the following worksheet to reflect on Becca's story and how it is similar or different from your experience.

## Reflecting on Becca's Story

What elements of Becca's story resonate with you? Is her experience familiar to you?

_____

_____

_____

Why do you think that the skill of contributing might help Becca become more self-compassionate?

_____

_____

_____

What wisdom from your own life would you share with Becca about contributing to others?

_____

_____

_____

During their next session, Becca's therapist asked her to write a short self-compassion script about how helping others was a way to show herself the compassion she desired in her life. Becca took a few days to think about the assignment and then wrote:

*For me, it's self-compassionate to treat others the way I want to be treated. Using the skill of contributing to others is also an important reflection of my values.*

*Helping others helps me help myself. Helping others reduces feelings of emptiness.*

What do you think about Becca's self-compassion script? Create your personalized self-compassion script to help you remember just how effective this skill can be.

_____

_____

_____

_____

_____

## • *Trevor's Story*

*Trevor came to therapy about six months after a breakup with his girlfriend of three years. He told his therapist that he thought that "nothing mattered anymore," felt like life was meaningless, and wondered whether his depressive episode would ever end. Trevor's therapist asked whether he could practice self-compassion around the ending of his relationship and Trevor responded by saying, "Are you kidding? The relationship ended because of me."*

*During Trevor's initial therapy assessment, his therapist noted that he lacked a lot of distress tolerance skills that may help him get through this depressive episode. The therapist told Trevor about dialectical behavior therapy and he was open to the idea of learning skills that could help him when his all-or-nothing thinking came up and he was tempted to imagine that he'd never feel better again.*

*Over the next several months, Trevor began to practice a skill or two each day and then would write a few sentences about how helpful the ideas were in alleviating some of his depression. He found that several skills were beneficial, while others didn't seem to make much of a difference in how he felt. His therapist observed this progress by noting, "This is great! You are figuring out what works and what doesn't. You are taking steps to help yourself feel better."*

*One day, Trevor and his therapist began to talk about the skill of contributing to others. Trevor admitted that he rarely took any steps to help others unless he was asked. He even argued that he felt too depressed to help others. His therapist gave him a homework assignment that week: Find an organization where he could volunteer for four or six hours a week. Trevor agreed to come up with an idea or two even though he didn't think this skill would help him.*

*That week, Trevor remembered that a work colleague talked about volunteering with a local first-generation college student mentorship program at the community college. Trevor had worked with a mentor as a freshman in college and believed that the experience helped set him up for success as a college student. A few days later, Trevor spoke with his colleague about the mentorship opportunity. Trevor would be asked to make a six-month commitment to helping just one student. Interestingly enough, Trevor was expected to volunteer for four or six hours a week—exactly what his therapist had suggested.*

*About a month later, Trevor was assigned to a student. He took the responsibility of mentorship seriously and found that he had a lot in common with the student. Soon he started looking forward to volunteering for just a few hours one evening a week. Trevor observed that on days when he volunteered, he felt less depressed and a little more hopeful. His therapist noted that he looked "lighter" and more confident once he started to volunteer. She also told Trevor that volunteering seemed to help him be a little more self-compassionate. He responded by saying, "Maybe. I mean, everyone needs help at some point in their lives, right? I benefited from having a mentor in college and now I'm doing the same for someone else. I guess it beats sitting at home feeling sorry for myself."*

Use the following worksheet to reflect on Trevor's story and how it is similar or different from your experience.

## Reflecting on Trevor's Story

What elements of Trevor's story are familiar to you?

_____

_____

_____

_____

Sometimes it's tempting to think that we don't have much to give others because of a diagnosis, set of symptoms, or the belief that this skill might help others but not us. List a few arguments for how helping others can be a way of increasing our self-compassion.

_____

_____

_____

Is there any other wisdom about contributing to others that you might want to share with Trevor?

_____

_____

_____

Trevor's therapist asked him to write a short self-compassion script about his experience in helping others as a way to help himself. Trevor took a couple of days to think about the assignment and then wrote:

> Volunteering has helped me get out of my own head and see that I have something valuable to give to a student in my community. While I may not have control over all of my emotions, I can always take steps to help myself when I'm feeling depressed. When I help others, I like myself more. My depression doesn't feel so big.
>
> Helping others is a way for me to be more self-compassionate.

What do you think about Trevor's self-compassion script? Is there anything else you might encourage him to think about or add to his script?

_____

_____

_____

_____

# Summary

- Altruism means that we find or create ways to help others.

- Contributing is a distress tolerance skill to help ourselves feel better as we help others.

- Contributing may also reduce feelings of emptiness and could be something that provides meaning and purpose.

- You can get ready to use this skill by generating dozens of ways in which you can engage in seemingly random acts of kindness.

- People who prioritize helping others are more likely to feel or experience self-compassion.

- All of us need a little extra help at some point in our lives.

- Don't make the mistake of waiting to contribute to others until you are "recovered" or feeling better. You might find that contributing to others may be the key piece of your recovery from borderline personality disorder.

Add your own ideas below.

- _____

- _____

CHAPTER 9

# Inappropriate, Intense Anger or Difficulty Controlling Anger

When I tell my clients, "Anger is a normal, healthy emotion that everyone experiences," they are often surprised. Many of the people I work with have been told or led to believe that anger is "bad" or "wrong," and that they should control angry emotions. It can be pretty invalidating to be told that how you feel is not how you should feel.

There is, however, a second part of my declaration, and that is, "The emotion is rarely the problem. It's the behaviors associated with the emotion."

Here's what it might look like:

- Being angry enough to throw the phone isn't the problem, but throwing the phone is problematic.

- Being offended enough to yell and say something mean isn't the problem, but yelling and saying mean things is problematic.

- Being outraged enough to throw a tantrum due to slow service at a restaurant isn't the problem, but throwing a tantrum in front of restaurant staff who are doing their best is problematic.

- Being annoyed by slow drivers isn't the problem, but honking your car's horn to get people to drive faster is problematic.

- Being frustrated with yourself when you make a mistake isn't the problem, but taking out the anger with self-sabotaging or self-destructive behaviors is problematic.

Can you see the difference? Because anger isn't an emotion we can always trust, we don't necessarily want to act on the emotion. Again, the emotion—all by itself—is rarely the problem, but your reaction to the emotion can get you in a lot of trouble. Complete the following worksheet to assess how prevalent this symptom is for you. This worksheet can also be found at http://www.newharbinger.com/55664.

## Assessing Anger and Intense Emotions

Has the experience of frustration, anger, or rage ever been a problem for you? How so?

_____

_____

_____

How has anger affected your relationships with others?

_____

_____

_____

Has your expression of anger prevented you from reaching important goals in your life?

_____

_____

_____

Understanding more about anger and your urges to act on intense emotion is a great first step. The next step is to get curious about your anger, because getting curious is another opportunity to practice self-compassion.

# Self-Compassion Skill: A Skillful Response to Anger

Anger is often referred to as a secondary emotion. That means that the primary emotion can be different, but what comes up or what other people see is the behavior associated with anger. Sometimes people will observe something like, "He's an angry person," but I don't think that's always accurate. It's true that we might see anger in ourselves and others, but there can be more to the story and a quick observation may not be enough. This is a terrific time to make the choice to respond to your anger with curiosity.

So, when anger comes up for me or for my clients, one of my first questions is: What's underneath the anger? Is it fear or sadness?

Asking this question often does a couple of different things. The first benefit is that we're allowing ourselves to be nonjudgmental and curious about the emotion. The second benefit is that the longer we stay nonjudgmental and curious about the emotion, the less likely we are to act on the emotion in a way that could be problematic for us or others.

Marsha Linehan (2015) writes about the DBT skill of being mindfully effective—or making a commitment to doing what works—in her skills training manual. Personally, it's one of my favorite skills because it gives us the room to ask ourselves, "Is this effective?" or, in other words, "Is this going to help me?" For instance, you could also ask yourself, "Will anger help or hurt?" or "Will I feel better if I say this mean thing out loud?" Pausing long enough (or by using the distress tolerance STOP skill discussed in chapter 5) to ask yourself these questions helps you understand more about what's happening inside so that you can make more effective decisions about what to do next.

Of course, anger can often be justified, so you may have a reason to be angry that makes sense to you or others. Anger may be beneficial when it leads to problem-solving, seeking justice, or protecting ourselves or others, but if anger is intense, it might be harder to be mindfully effective. That's why it can be healthy to explore what's underneath the anger. That mindful and purposeful exploration can make anger more manageable in a pretty short amount of time.

The following worksheet lists a few situations where fear or sadness might be masked by anger. The situations described aren't meant to dismiss anger or expressions of anger but to illustrate that there might be something more that's happening. Can you allow yourself to be curious about what might be underneath the anger? You might be able to argue for the emotions of both fear and sadness when you think about each situation. There's no "right" or "wrong" answer. You may not be certain, but give yourself permission to make an educated guess based on your own wisdom. This worksheet can also be found at http://www.newharbinger.com/55664.

## Exploring What Is Beneath the Anger

Jessie usually gets a "sweet dreams" text from her boyfriend between 10:00 p.m. and midnight. This specific text means a lot to her. One night when she didn't hear from him by 12:20 a.m., she became confused. Jessie started to cry and then felt nauseous. She called his phone about a dozen times and left several tearful and threatening voice messages and texts.

Do you think that Jessie felt more fear or sadness when she didn't hear from her boyfriend during the time when he usually reached out? What else could be going on for her?

_____

_____

_____

Augustus was incredulous when he saw that his manager scheduled him to work on a specific weekend he had asked to have off so he could celebrate his wedding anniversary. Feeling confused and frustrated, he told his wife, "This is so disrespectful. I'm a good employee and I scheduled this vacation time almost three months ago. It was approved by management. I should quit and go somewhere I'll be more appreciated."

Do you think that Augustus felt more fear or sadness when he saw that he was scheduled to work during a time when he was supposed to be celebrating his anniversary? What else could be going on for him?

_____

_____

_____

Greg reached out to a friend and former work colleague on Monday morning via text about getting lunch and catching up. On Friday morning Greg still hadn't heard back but then noticed that his colleague was active on Facebook and had just announced the birth of his first child. Greg was happy for his colleague but also felt a little annoyed that he found out on Facebook. Greg thought to himself, "I thought we were better friends than that."

Do you think that Greg felt more fear or sadness when he saw his colleague's announcement on Facebook? What else could be going on for him?

_____

_____

_____

Jenn's partner Sam was almost an hour late coming home from work. When she tried to check his location, it looked like his phone may have been turned off. She tried calling him but got no response. With each passing minute, Jenn angrily paced in front of their house and rehearsed how she would tell Sam that he was thoughtless and selfish for not keeping his phone charged. After another half hour, Jenn got a call from the sheriff's department. Sam had been in a multi-car accident and was being taken to a nearby hospital for observation.

Do you think that Jenn felt more fear or sadness when it looked like Sam's phone had been turned off and she couldn't reach him? What else could be going on for her?

_____

_____

_____

When we acknowledge to ourselves and others the emotions that are underneath the anger, it can be a sign that we are also being self-compassionate. In essence, we are communicating to ourselves what's really happening—without any kind of self-judgment, shame, embarrassment, or condemnation.

What's the end result of responding to our anger with curiosity and acknowledging underlying fear or sadness? From the situations described in the worksheet, it might sound like this:

- The next day, Jessie reflected "I thought that my boyfriend had probably fallen asleep early but I wasn't certain. I wish that I had named the fear and had practiced some self-soothing to reduce my anxiety before I did something I regretted."

- Later that evening, Augustus told his wife, "It's not just about the mix-up with the schedule. I don't always feel appreciated at work in the way I'd like. Naming the fear of being disrespected is a way for me to acknowledge that I was hurt without quitting my job or doing something else that will get me fired."

- A few hours later, Greg told himself, "Friendships mean a lot to me and I want to know that I also matter to those I care about. It hurts when that doesn't happen and, at the same time, it makes sense why I didn't hear from my friend this week."

- When Jenn rushed to the hospital, Sam told her, "Everything happened so quickly and I couldn't find the phone to tell you what happened. The first responders assured me that someone would call you soon. I knew you'd be worried." Jenn admitted that she felt angry when she couldn't see Sam's location but that her anger turned to fear when she got the call from emergency services. She thought to herself, "I'm so thankful that Sam's alive. I wonder why I got so angry in the first place."

Jessie, Augustus, Greg, and Jenn all increased their capacity to respond to their emotional pain with much-needed self-compassion.

If anger is a secondary emotion for you and you pause long enough to ask yourself, "What's underneath this anger?" what do you think is usually true for you? Do you think you experience more fear or sadness?

_____

_____

_____

_____

_____

## How to Use This Skill

We can use this skill of being mindfully effective and doing what works by asking ourselves a lot of questions and being curious about the emotional experience of anger. For instance, would it be mindfully effective to:

- Yell and scream for a manager in the middle of a store?

- End a decades-long friendship when you didn't receive an invitation to a birthday party?

- Leave an abusive restaurant review when they took a favorite meal off the menu?

- Ghost someone over a misunderstanding that led to an argument?

- Threaten to have someone fired if they don't quickly process a refund?

- Refuse to forgive a family member when they've asked for forgiveness?

Again, you may have legitimate and justified reasons for being angry. Validating those reasons to yourself may be an act of self-compassion, especially if you aren't used to honoring your self-respect. Other times, however, anger may not be justified or you may not want to act on your anger. Ultimately, you get to decide what is most effective for you.

The following worksheet will help you explore your anger and make mindfully effective choices before problematic behavior kicks in. This worksheet can also be found at http://www.newharbinger.com/55664.

## Finding Effective Ways to Cope with Anger

What are some healthier, more effective way to express or talk about justified anger?

_____

_____

_____

How often are you self-validating the emotion of anger? Explore your reasons for validating or not validating your anger.

_____

_____

_____

Try using the sentence prompt mentioned in chapter 3 of "It makes sense that I feel angry because ..."

_____

_____

_____

## • *Kessa's Story*

*Kessa was in her early thirties when she was told by yet another partner that she had anger issues she needed to learn how to control.*

*Most of the time, Kessa didn't understand her own emotional reactions and she usually felt embarrassed and full of shame when she acted out on her anger. On more than one occasion,* people in stores or restaurants backed away from Kessa when she was having an anger episode. As someone who often felt lonely and longed for connection, Kessa was horrified to realize that people sometimes described her as an angry or out-of-control woman. One of her worst fears was that she would lose control in public and someone would record her and post the video on social media.

Relationship after relationship would end when a boyfriend would say something to the effect of, "You've got to get your anger under control. I love you, but I can't be with someone who is this angry all the time." Kessa knew this was true but didn't know how to understand her anger or how she could help herself when she felt angry.

A friend referred Kessa to a therapist who specialized in self-compassion. When her boyfriend heard this, he responded by dismissively saying, "That's ridiculous. Self-compassion is not going to solve your anger problems. You need to be harder on yourself and just stop doing this."

Kessa's therapist explained that telling people to stop engaging in a particular behavior rarely worked. Instead, the therapist asked Kessa to talk about what was underneath her anger. She wondered whether Kessa felt more sadness or fear. As soon as Kessa heard the question, she began to cry and shared her how she felt deeply unlovable to others. Kessa said, "If others can't love me, how can I love myself? I think that the anger is often an act of desperation. I want to feel something, but my sadness is too much for most people. My boyfriend doesn't know what to do when I cry. With anger, I get a response. It's not one I like, but it's better than nothing."

Over the next several months, Kessa slowly shared her life story with her therapist. She noticed that talking about the sadness and losses she experienced in her life slowly reduced the anger she felt. Her therapist told her, "There's an important connection between your anger and sadness. We're connecting the dots together."

Kessa's therapist also introduced her to the DBT skill of being mindfully effective and doing what worked. With this skill, Kessa learned more about observing and describing her emotions while asking herself, "Is it helping me to act out on this anger I'm feeling?" She noticed that if she mindfully observed and described her sadness often enough, her emotional experience felt more manageable and less scary. She was no longer "out of control." For her, slowing things down so that she could ask herself, "What's really happening in this moment?" also became a way for her to practice self-compassion. After a few more months, Kessa said to her therapist, "The more self-compassionate I am, the less sadness and anger I feel. I didn't think that it would work for me, but it does."

Use the following worksheet to reflect on Kessa's story and how it is similar or different from your experience.

# Reflecting on Kessa's Story

What elements of Kessa's story feel familiar to you?

_____

_____

_____

Being mindfully effective means doing what works in the moment. What worked for Kessa when it came to understanding and experiencing her anger?

_____

_____

_____

Other people in your life may think that self-condemnation can be a way to control anger. What advice would you give to a friend who believed this?

_____

_____

_____

During their final session together, Kessa's therapist asked her to write a short self-compassion script about how being mindfully effective and curious about her anger could be an act of self-compassion. That night Kessa wrote in her journal:

_There's a reason why I feel and act the way I do. I'm not defined by my anger, but I need skills to cope with the anger I have._

_Getting in touch with my sadness helps me respond to my emotional pain in a more self-loving and self-compassionate way. I stay in control when I commit to doing what works._

_If I can love myself in this way, others can also love me._

Kessa made an important observation when she noticed, "The more self-compassionate I am, the less sadness and anger I feel. I didn't think that it would work for me, but it does." Why do you think this might be true for her?

_____

_____

_____

_____

_____

## • *Noah's Story*

*Noah was in his mid-thirties when he was referred to treatment by the court after a domestic dispute with his girlfriend ended in mutual violence.*

*Noah told his therapist that he was glad that he got arrested. He explained, "I knew that I needed help for years. I felt like it was just a matter of time before something happened. I couldn't ask for help because I didn't know what to say without sounding like a crazy person. I thought I would be told to just 'stop it.'" He tearfully added, "I can't control my anger. I don't know how to control this part of myself. I hate who I am and how I've hurt others."*

*Noah's therapist helped him by explaining that it can be beneficial to ask, "What is underneath the anger? Is it sadness or fear?" He also introduced Noah to the DBT skill of being mindfully effective, and he asked Noah to start tracking the emotions of anger, sadness, fear, shame, and guilt every day. When an emotion came up, Noah set the timer on his phone for one minute and explored the emotions without self-judgment. If they could uncover some emotional patterns over an extended period of time, Noah's therapist was confident that Noah could consistently help reduce his anger responses.*

*Over a period of several months, Noah could see that a pattern of emotions and behaviors began to emerge. With lots of information, Noah could see that anger was often associated with a fear of not being able to control something that, in the moment, felt uncontrollable. The fear of loss of control came up at work, with misunderstandings among friends, and in his romantic relationships. Noah's therapist observed, "So fear is the primary emotion, but it comes out as anger, right?" Noah agreed and pointed to almost a decade of stories where intense fear seemed to come out as anger.*

*In treatment, Noah continued to track his emotions, but their sessions were now primarily focused on recognizing and responding to Noah's fear in a more skillful way. Noah's therapist not only taught him the effectiveness skill but also DBT skills like self-soothing and radical acceptance to help Noah create healthier relationships with those he loved. He also shared a self-compassion meditation that Noah could listen to each morning on his way to work. Noah noticed that when he used his skills every day, he felt less fear and, therefore, experienced less anger.*

Use the following worksheet to reflect on Noah's story and how it is similar or different from your experience.

## Reflecting on Noah's Story

What elements of Noah's story resonate with you?

_____

_____

_____

How did being mindfully effective help Noah understand that reacting from a place of anger wasn't helping him feel more in control of his life or his relationships?

_____

_____

_____

Do you have any ideas about why a self-compassionate approach in treatment worked so well for Noah? Why do you think it reduced his self-hatred?

_____

_____

_____

At their one-year anniversary of working together, Noah's therapist asked him to write a short self-compassion script about how effective it was for him to respond to his emotions with more self-compassion. Noah wrote:

> *Understanding what's underneath my anger has helped change my life. If I can use the skill of being mindfully effective and focus on what is most helpful, I won't act out on the anger and I can respond to my fear in a healthier way. I don't have to hate myself because of my anger or fear.*
>
> *I can now be a more self-compassionate person who has healthy relationships with others. I'm not the man I was a year ago.*

What do you think about Noah's self-compassion script? Create your own self-compassion script for the skill of being mindfully effective to help reduce anger in your life.

_____

_____

_____

_____

_____

# Summary

- Anger is a normal emotion that everyone experiences at one time or another.

- Telling someone to control their anger or just "let it go" is rarely helpful.

- The emotion of anger may not be the problem, but the actions associated with the anger may be problematic.

- You may not be an angry person but you may be someone who experiences anger.

- Asking yourself, "What's underneath this anger?" is an invitation to be more aware of the role of anger in your life. That willingness to explore the emotion can help you become more self-compassionate.

- The DBT skill of being mindfully effective helps you focus on what works. It's the opposite of engaging in your action urge for anger.

- Developing a personalized self-compassion script may help you cope more effectively when you experience anger.

Add your own ideas below.

- _____

- _____

# CHAPTER 10

# Paranoia or Dissociation

The last diagnostic criterion according to the *DSM-5* (APA 2013) for borderline personality disorder is paranoia and dissociative symptoms. Complete the following worksheet to assess how prevalent this symptom is for you. This worksheet can also be found at http://www.newharbinger.com/55664.

## Assessing Paranoia and Dissociation

Check off any of the following that you have experienced either recently or in the past.

### Paranoia

☐ You feel like you can't trust others.

☐ You believe that others may want to hurt you.

☐ You think that people may be lying to you.

☐ You experience a pattern of distrust or suspiciousness.

☐ You think that you are being threatened by others.

☐ You think that others are spying on or watching you.

☐ You feel attacked by others when no real threat exists.

## Dissociation

☐  You feel physically disconnected or separate from your surroundings.

☐  You experience temporary immobility or feeling "frozen."

☐  You feel like you are stuck in a dreamlike state.

☐  You experience short-term memory loss or lose time after an episode of acute stress.

☐  You feel like you are not fully present in your own body.

☐  You are not able to speak or respond to others for short periods of time.

In the space below, explore any ways in which you may have experienced paranoia or dissociation as a symptom of borderline personality disorder.

_____

_____

_____

Diagnosing both paranoia and dissociation can sometimes be challenging even for experienced mental health professionals. If you aren't certain whether these symptoms apply to you, I want to encourage you to ask for a complete assessment with an experienced health care professional—a psychiatrist, psychiatric nurse, nurse practitioner, psychologist, clinical social worker, or licensed counselor who is qualified to diagnose paranoia or dissociation. When diagnosing for paranoia and dissociation symptoms, a health care professional will want to rule out psychotic disorders, anxiety disorders, the effects of current or past drug use, alcohol abuse, other personality disorders, or a medical condition that may explain some or all of the symptoms.

We know that for most people with a diagnosis of borderline personality disorder, acute or overwhelming stress can make these symptoms worse. Paranoia and dissociation may also be caused by abuse, neglect, memories or reminders about past abuse or neglect, acts of violence, bullying, or other trauma.

The good news is that making a commitment to regularly using your DBT skills can greatly reduce the intensity or duration of paranoia or dissociation. You might be someone who finds that once you manage stress effectively, these symptoms are rare. While you may not be able to perfectly control when and how these symptoms appear, excellent self-care (which includes your commitment to being self-compassionate) will help when you are extra vulnerable to paranoia or dissociation.

Of course, not everyone with a diagnosis of borderline personality disorder will have these symptoms; most individuals may only experience some symptoms during periods of high stress or during an emergency. Again, this is something an experienced mental health professional will be able to accurately diagnose. Your health care professional will also want to know more about your family's medical history, when your symptoms began, and how these symptoms may have affected your ability to work, attend school, or experience healthy relationships.

Here are a few examples of how paranoia and dissociation might look for some individuals:

- As a child, Joan's family home was lost to a fire. Neither Joan nor any family members were harmed in the fire but a beloved pet dog, Lucy, died as a result of her injuries as she was being rescued. Years later, when Joan sees a dog that looks similar to Lucy, she will often tear up and then become "frozen" for up to five minutes. Recently she explained to her therapist that when this happens, she sometimes feels like she's in the middle of a dream and cannot make herself wake up.

- Christopher grew up in a home where a caregiver abused alcohol daily. As an adult, he found it difficult to trust others and told his therapist that he thought that the people at his workplace were bullying new employees and several managers were out to take advantage of him as well as other workers. While he admitted that his theory may not be perfectly accurate, he told his therapist, "I don't assume that anyone is ever good. People have to earn my trust. It's not guaranteed."

- When Marc was in college, he witnessed a fatal shooting outside a bar. Almost a decade later, Marc is still sensitive to sudden loud noises that sound like "bangs" or "pops." One recent evening, a neighbor started to light firecrackers as part of a birthday celebration. Marc responded to the noise by freezing and sinking to the bedroom floor. When his wife asked, "Marc, what happened? What's wrong?" Marc found that he couldn't speak for almost ten minutes.

Educating yourself about paranoia and dissociation is important for healing and recovery. For my clients who want to learn more about this particular set of symptoms, I recommend *Coping with Trauma-Related Dissociation: Skills Training for Patients and Therapists* by Suzette Boon, Kathy Steele, and Onno Van der Hart (W. W. Norton, 2011). The ideas and skills found in this book are wholly compatible with the skills you'll find in dialectical behavior therapy.

If you have been diagnosed with a psychotic disorder or a mood disorder with psychotic symptoms, I highly recommend the book *The Dialectical Behavior Therapy Skills Workbook for Psychosis: Manage Your Emotions, Reduce Symptoms, and Get Back to Your Life* by Maggie Mullen (New Harbinger, 2021). I believe that it will be an excellent addition to the DBT skills work you are already learning and using in treatment.

*Note:* Please remember to ask your health care provider about these particular symptoms of borderline personality disorder. Do not try to self-diagnose paranoia or dissociation.

# Self-Compassion Skill: Becoming Mindfully Nonjudgmental

When many people experience paranoia or dissociation as a symptom of borderline personality disorder, it's often followed by feelings of shame or embarrassment. What's important to recognize is that these symptoms don't start in a vacuum. That means there's a cause you can usually identify and then you have a choice to respond to these symptoms without judging yourself. This is what Marsha Linehan (2015) calls the powerful skill of taking a nonjudgmental stance or being committed to approaching life nonjudgmentally.

If you've ever had an urge to judge yourself when you noticed symptoms of borderline personality disorder, you are not alone. Many people with a diagnosis of borderline personality disorder have a critical, condemning, or judgmental inner voice. You might even be someone who says to themselves, "I'm a bad friend," or "I'm never going to change. Life will always be difficult." When it comes to symptoms of paranoia and dissociation, you might also notice that you are judging your emotions, reactions, or experience.

How do you recognize a judgmental thought? Usually it contains a descriptor like "good," "bad," "awful," "never," "always," "perfect," "better," or "worse." In essence, it's a shorthand way of using the observe and describe skills that we covered earlier in this book. The problem is that you may sometimes get stuck in your judgmental thinking and imagine that the judgments are true. Judgments can also keep your emotions high and intense, making them harder to manage.

It can be interesting to understand just how self-judgmental you are. Indicate whether any of the following are, or have been, true for you.

☐ *I have a tendency to blame myself when I'm having a difficult day.*

☐ *I judge myself before others blame me.*

☐ *I overemphasize my flaws or mistakes.*

☐ *I don't like it when others suggest, "Just forgive yourself and move on."*

☐ *I rarely "let it go" when it comes to things I hate about myself.*

☐ *Not liking myself is part of who I am.*

☐ *I sometimes tell myself that I'm not really getting better and that it's just a delusion.*

☐ *I need to be perfect.*

☐ *Others won't like me if I don't change.*

☐ *It's natural for me to be hard on myself.*

☐ *I think about my problems all the time.*

☐ *I don't like who I am even though I've made lots of progress.*

☐ *My inner voice is really mean and often cruel.*

You may have already noticed that being self-judgmental is the opposite of self-compassion. Self-judgment keeps you from creating a life worth living. It keeps you from being connected to others. It whispers "you can't" when you really can. This is why self-compassion is such an important emotional health skill to develop.

When I'm teaching this idea to my clients, I often explain something like, "Marsha Linehan doesn't want you to be a robot and never have any judgments about anything ever again." The goal in learning and using this skill is to help you turn down the volume on those judgments that keep you stuck in patterns that aren't helping you be the person you want to be.

Paranoia and dissociation can cloud your judgment. It's one thing to experience the symptoms, but if you start to judge the symptom or the experience, you potentially make your life more challenging just because of your self-judgments. Many people also find that after they engage in self-judgments, they experience additional shame, guilt, or embarrassment. They might also feel emotionally or physically exhausted just from judging themselves. These self-judgments can also fuel depressive or anxiety symptoms or lead to self-harm behaviors or suicidal thinking for many people with a diagnosis of borderline personality disorder. Therefore, it's even more important to practice self-compassion and a nonjudgmental stance.

If you've noticed that changing the emotions you have about yourself can be a battle, you're not alone. Self-judgments are easy. Challenging those judgments and finding the truth is hard. As with all of these ideas, the goal isn't to become a "perfect" person who never has judgments. Instead, you might nonjudgmentally (and accurately) say:

• I sometimes experience paranoia, but I'm not a paranoid person.

or

• I sometimes experience symptoms of dissociation, but these symptoms don't define who I am as a person.

# How to Use This Skill

There are many ways we can recognize and change our self-judgments. The first step is to recognize a judgment for what it is—something that is not true or only partially true, and something that keeps you stuck in unwanted thoughts and emotions. You might look for all-or-nothing words like "good," "bad," "right," or "wrong" as clues that you may be making judgments about yourself or others.

You can even check in with friends or your therapist if you aren't sure whether a thought is a judgment. For example, you might call a friend and ask, "I'm trying to be more mindful of my judgments and just found that I was telling myself that I'm not going to get better. I was talking myself out of going to my DBT skills group tonight. Do you think that might be a judgment?"

Next, you can focus on what's true or accurate. You might acknowledge that you don't think you'll get better, but you also know that you can't always trust your thoughts. It might be true that getting better is really hard and may take time, but it's probably not true that you won't see any improvement from learning and practicing these skills.

Finally, make room for some self-compassion. You could tell yourself, "It's hard to undo these thoughts that have been a part of my life for many years. I would never tell a friend that he couldn't get better, so why would I say that to myself when I've been working so hard at making lasting changes?"

The following worksheet will help you explore this idea of taking a nonjudgmental stance toward your symptoms. This worksheet can also be found at http://www.newharbinger.com/55664.

## Exploring Nonjudgment

What do you think about the idea of separating the symptom or set of symptoms from your self-judgments? Has this ever been a problem for you?

_____

_____

_____

What would your life look like if you judged yourself just 10 or 15 percent less than you do now? Stay curious as you write about what your life might be like with fewer self-judgments.

_____

_____

_____

What are some ways you might be able to use the skill of being mindfully nonjudgmental?

_____

_____

_____

You might only see results from using this skill when you commit to a consistent, daily practice. What are some obstacles that may prevent you from practicing this skill?

_____

_____

_____

How can you overcome these obstacles so that you can practice the skill of being mindfully nonjudgmental?

_____

_____

_____

## • *Rachel's Story*

*Rachel was diagnosed with borderline personality disorder and post-traumatic stress disorder (PTSD) in her early thirties. She had been in treatment off and on for half of her life when a therapist helped her see the potential connection between the two diagnoses. It was true that not everyone with a diagnosis of borderline personality disorder experiences trauma, but for many individuals like Rachel, acknowledging this part of her history was an important step in her healing. It was a key part of the treatment plan she developed with her therapist, who specialized in DBT-Prolonged Exposure (Harned 2022), an evidence-based treatment that combines dialectical behavior therapy with prolonged exposure for the treatment of trauma.*

*When Rachel was initially talking to her therapist about her goals in treatment, she discussed feelings of self-hatred and self-disgust. When her therapist asked her about self-judgments, Rachel* said, "Yes, I know that I'm judging myself all the time. Even when I dissociate, I judge myself later. I think, 'Yeah, that was embarrassing. Don't do that again.'"

Rachel's therapist talked about the benefits of being nonjudgmental and how it would also give her the room she needed to respond to her symptoms with more self-compassion and kindness. Together, Rachel and her therapist came up with a plan for Rachel to track the judgmental thoughts she was having toward herself. Over many weeks, a fairly predictable pattern began to unfold. When Rachel experienced a lot of stress and was more prone to dissociating, the event was preceded and then followed by more self-judgmental thoughts.

Rachel's therapist said, "If we could reduce your judgmental thoughts and self-talk, I wonder if we could decrease the number of times during the week when you experience dissociation." Rachel wasn't certain this would help but was willing to try. Much to her surprise, Rachel noticed that if she could respond to her emotional pain with greater self-compassion, she was less likely to dissociate. During the times when she did experience a dissociative episode, she felt like she had more control. She also observed that the episodes were less intense and didn't last as long.

After three months of careful tracking of these new skills and behaviors, Rachel told her therapist, "Practicing being nonjudgmental makes a difference when I can remember to do it. It was harder at first, but then it became easier. I find myself thinking, 'This is a judgment. I don't have to entertain it. It's not who I am.'"

Use the following worksheet to reflect on Rachel's story and how it is similar or different from your experience.

## Reflecting on Rachel's Story

What elements of Rachel's story resonate with you?

_____

_____

_____

_____

How did the skill of being mindfully nonjudgmental help Rachel become more self-compassionate?

_____

_____

_____

How can the skill of being mindfully nonjudgmental help you become more self-compassionate?

_____

_____

_____

Rachel's therapist encouraged her to create a self-compassion script about letting go of the self-judgments that have kept her stuck in patterns that are not a part of Rachel's life worth living. The next week, Rachel returned to treatment with her script. She wrote:

> *The judgments I was making about myself and my diagnoses kept me in self-destructive patterns. When trauma memories return, I can respond by being factual about what's happening. I can choose to be kind to myself.*
>
> *Turning toward a nonjudgmental stance allows me to become more self-compassionate.*

What do you think of Rachel's self-compassion script? Write a similar script about what is important for you to remember when stress is overwhelming or intense.

_____

_____

_____

_____

_____

- *Emma's Story*

Shortly after she dropped out of college in her senior year, Emma started treatment with a therapist who specialized in working with individuals who are emotionally sensitive.

Emma had been raised in an environment where her caregivers were not always responsible nor trustworthy. As a result, Emma often found it difficult to trust others as an adult. In relationship after relationship, Emma found it hard to connect with others in a way that felt healthy and meaningful. When misunderstandings and hurt feelings surfaced for Emma, she would often push others away. She explained to her therapist, "I can't be hurt again. Sometimes I think everyone will hurt me. I can make myself paranoid thinking, 'Who will hurt me next?' I'm quite obsessive about it."

Emma's therapist assessed her for relational patterns throughout her life that kept her from connecting the way she really desired. After a few sessions, she asked Emma, "Do you judge yourself or others more?" Emma quickly said, "I'm definitely harder on myself. My paranoid thoughts are mean. I think that I'm unlovable or that I'm disgusting. If I see it in myself, others have to believe it's also true. That might sound ridiculous, but that's how I think."

That's when Emma's therapist told her about the skill of taking a nonjudgmental stance. She explained that people have judgments about themselves or others and that those judgments aren't necessarily true, but we often act like they are. She explained, "Many emotionally sensitive people have more judgments about themselves than they have judgments about others. I wonder what your life would be like if you could reduce those self-judgmental thoughts. What if you could become a more self-compassionate person?"

Emma left the session intrigued by the idea. No one had ever suggested that reducing her self-judgments might help her cope with the emotional pain she had been experiencing for a long time.

The next session, Emma's therapist talked more about reducing self-judgments as a way to become more self-compassionate. She asked if Emma was open to creating a journal of her self-judgments so that they could talk about how she could reduce those judgments and focus more on what was true. Emma said that she was willing to do that for the next seven days.

Emma went home and started a list. At the end of the week, she had over a hundred self-judgmental statements to work on in treatment. As she looked over the list before her next session, Emma thought about her therapist's question: What would her life be like if she could reduce these judgments and become a more self-compassionate person?

She took the question seriously and told herself, "If I were more self-compassionate, I wouldn't have dropped out of school. I wouldn't be self-sabotaging. I wouldn't be so afraid. My paranoia about being hurt by others wouldn't be so overwhelming."

It sounded like a nice idea to Emma.

*In session, Emma's therapist asked her to go through each statement (the first one was, "I'm unlovable") and ask herself, "Is this true? How do I know it's true?" Over time, Emma was able to find a balance between what she insisted was true and the statements that were not true. Emma's therapist would ask, "Is there a kernel of truth here? What is it? Look for the evidence."*

*About six months later, Emma told her therapist that this had been one of the most helpful DBT skills she had learned in treatment. It was so effective that she continued to write a few sentences reflecting on three to five self-judgmental statements each day.*

Use the following worksheet to reflect on Emma's story and how it is similar or different from your experience.

## Reflecting on Emma's Story

What parts of Emma's story resonated with you?

_____

_____

_____

How could you take steps to become less self-judgmental? Would Emma's method of listing her self-judgments be something you could do? What else might be helpful for you?

_____

_____

_____

Becoming a less self-judgmental person was a big goal for Emma. What advice would you have for a friend who struggles with self-judgments?

_____

_____

_____

Emma's therapist then asked her to write a self-compassion script about what she learned about reducing her self-judgments. Emma wrote:

*I've been so judgmental of myself in the past. I'm still judgmental of myself today, but I recognize when I'm judging myself.*

*Letting go of the judgments helps me be more self-compassionate. I'm a healthier me when I can be kind to myself. This is a way for me to love myself as I continue to heal.*

What do you think of the self-compassion script that Emma created? Is there anything else you might add to the script?

_____

_____

_____

_____

_____

_____

## Summary

- Check in with a qualified mental health professional about symptoms related to paranoia or dissociation. This is not an area you want to self-diagnose. Talk to an expert.

- Self-judgment is the opposite of self-compassion.

- The DBT skill of being mindfully nonjudgmental is designed to help you reduce the self-judgments that are preventing you from creating a life worth living.

- Recognizing judgments about your diagnosis or symptoms related to borderline personality disorder is your first step to reducing those judgments.

- When you say to yourself, "I don't have to judge myself right now," or "This is a judgment. I can let it go," you have a greater capacity to respond to your emotional pain with greater kindness.

- Consistently tracking self-judgments will help you to see your progress over long periods of time.

- Engaging in self-compassionate self-talk or acts is a choice we make to help ourselves.

Add your own ideas below.

- _____

- _____

# CHAPTER 11

# Bringing the Self-Compassionate Ideas and Skills Together

Hooray! You made it to the final chapter of this book.

So are you now self-compassionate? Are you making a choice to love yourself when you feel unlovable? Are you lovingly responding to all of your unwanted emotions? Have you let go of self-sabotaging behaviors in favor of self-love? Did you quickly embrace self-compassion when you made a mistake earlier today or said that thing that left you cringing?

No? Me, neither.

I would guess that for almost 100 percent of readers, these skills—although they make sense and usually work—can still be hard to regularly implement. That may be true for people with a diagnosis of borderline personality disorder and those who do not have a diagnosis of borderline personality disorder. These ideas or skills are for all of us. I have a hard time finding any exceptions.

Here's what my dear friend Debbie Corso observed about self-compassion in her book *Stronger Than BPD: The Girl's Guide to Taking Control of Intense Emotions, Drama, and Chaos Using DBT* (2017): "We are all tasked with lovingly and patiently teaching ourselves these skills as adults, and we can and do make positive differences in our lives by doing so—one step at a time, one practice at a time, one skillful distraction at a time—to prevent ourselves from making things worse."

Like Debbie and so many other people in your life, you may be a beautiful work in progress.

The goal isn't to become a perfectly self-compassionate person at any given moment. A healthy and realistic goal may look like expanding your capacity to be self-compassionate over a period of years or even decades.

## • *Madison's Story*

*Madison sat down on her therapist's couch and tearfully announced, "I did it again." "Did what again? What happened?" her therapist asked.*

*"I did everything. I think that I undid months of work in just a few days. I got so frustrated and I either forgot every skill I've learned in here or I got stubborn and refused to use the skills or ask for help. Just when I thought that I was done making a bad situation worse, I yelled at my best friend, threw my phone and broke it, and lied to my boss about completing a project I haven't even started yet. It was like that old book—Alexander and the* Terrible, Horrible, No Good, Very Bad Day *(Viorst 1987)—except that it lasted for two days. I seriously couldn't stop myself."*

*When Madison was done sharing the full story of what happened over the previous two days, her therapist validated her and then observed, "You could continue to beat yourself up or this might be a perfect opportunity to choose self-compassion." Madison replied, "I don't know how. I've made a big mess of everything," and started crying again.*

*Madison's therapist asked her to take out a blank DBT diary card so that they could come up with a plan together. She asked, "You're here in my office, so I'm going to say that you're being mindfully effective and are doing what works. What other skills could help you be just a little more compassionate toward yourself this afternoon?"*

*Madison listed a few skills like self-soothing with sound and touch, letting go of self-judgments, and radical acceptance. Together they talked about how Madison could use these skills over the next day.*

*Toward the end of their session, Madison's therapist asked her, "Can you forgive yourself for being human and having a rough couple of days?" Madison replied that she wasn't certain, but on her drive home she thought about the "terrible, horrible, no good, very bad" days she had before she ever heard of DBT and thought about how she was now armed with tools to help her have fewer rough days. Hating herself wasn't going to help. Forgiving herself for taking a half-step backward was probably a way to be self-compassionate.*

*After reviewing Madison's diary card that next week, Madison's therapist pointed out how many skills she used and reached out for a fist bump to celebrate. "Way to go! What helped you the most when you left my office last week?" Madison responded by saying, "I don't know if there was any one thing but I kept thinking that I was better off using some skills rather than no skills. I also remember you saying that I could forgive myself for being human. Everyone has a bad day, but I have a choice to be kind to myself."*

Use the following worksheet to reflect on Madison's story and how it is similar or different from your experience.

# Reflecting on Madison's Story

What elements of Madison's story feel familiar to you?

_____

_____

_____

How do difficult days sometimes create a self-compassion challenge for you?

_____

_____

_____

It's tempting to think that life may become easier and that you won't need a self-compassion practice in the future. What would it look like to be someone who commits to daily self-compassion for the rest of their life?

_____

_____

_____

_____

Madison's therapist encouraged her to create a self-compassion script the next time she felt discouraged about having a rough day or for those times when she reverted to previous ways of coping. The next week, Madison came to therapy with her script. She read to her therapist:

*I am a normal human being. I make mistakes and I'm never going to be perfect.*

*Treating myself with kindness helps me get back on track. Choosing self-compassion isn't just for other people. It's something I can choose for myself.*

What do you think of Madison's self-compassion script? What stands out to you as particularly effective?

_____

_____

_____

_____

_____

Write a self-compassion script for your own "terrible, horrible, no good, very bad day." What's most important for you to remember on your most challenging days? Consider sharing your script with a trusted and validating person in your life.

_____

_____

_____

_____

_____

## • *Connor's Story*

*Connor had been working with a therapist who specialized in self-compassion for the past six months. Over that period of time, Connor noticed that his self-hatred lessened. He was even able to identify a few times when he could respond to his emotional pain with some neutrality or even a little self-kindness. It wasn't easy, but even his best friend, Hannah, noticed a difference. She recently told Connor, "You're less negative and critical. Before you started treatment, it was really hard to be around you."*

*The next week, two life-changing events took place. Connor was laid off along with a dozen other employees at his office and his mother was diagnosed with a stage 4 cancer—even with aggressive treatment, she wasn't expected to live more than a year.*

*When he told his therapist the news, he said, "I knew it. Things were going too well. Even Hannah noticed the difference in me, but I hate my life. This kind of stuff always happens. Self-compassion isn't going to help me now." During what was a difficult session, Connor's therapist gave him a lot of room to talk about all of his fears for his future but also for his family's future. She didn't have any advice or wisdom for Connor that day—just a lot of validation and compassion.*

*The next day, Connor couldn't stop thinking about what Hannah had said recently. It was true that he hadn't been as negative or critical of others. It wasn't just Hannah who had noticed. Connor felt it too. He had changed. Choosing to be self-compassionate had made a difference over these past few months. He remembered what his therapist said about self-compassion being a choice he could return to again and again. Still, he couldn't see how he could practice what he learned in therapy now that his life was coming undone. He asked himself, "I don't know what will happen next. What if things get worse?"*

*When he saw his therapist again, he shared his thoughts and asked, "What am I missing? How am I supposed to practice self-compassion now?" Connor's therapist said that she wasn't exactly sure but wondered if it might sound something like, "This is what it's like to be an emotionally sensitive human in a hurting world. There are no easy answers when life hurts." She encouraged him to nonjudgmentally feel whatever it was that he needed to feel during this stressful time of his life.*

*Then she said, "Tell me what you would say to Hannah if she came to you with similar news." He answered honestly by saying, "At first, I'd probably try to distract her or cheer her up, but what she would probably want is for me to just be there for her." Connor's therapist agreed that was probably true. She observed, "Sitting quietly with our emotional pain is some of the hardest work we'll ever do. It's a powerful act of self-compassion."*

Use the following worksheet to reflect on Connor's story and how it is similar or different from your experience.

# Reflecting on Connor's Story

There are many days when we don't have a clear understanding about how to practice self-compassion. Some ideas might work for some people but not for others. If you had a friend like Connor, what wisdom from your own life would you want to share with him? Have you experienced a similar crisis? What helped you survive that period of your life?

_____

_____

_____

It can be tempting to judge our experiences, others, and ourselves. Why do you think Connor's therapist encouraged him to experience his emotions nonjudgmentally?

_____

_____

_____

Self-compassion researcher and author Kristin Neff (2011) recognizes that there is a "common humanity" component to a self-compassion practice. She means that it may help us to remember that we aren't alone in our pain or suffering. Acknowledging that we aren't the only ones hurting may be a way for us to be compassionate with ourselves. What do you think about the idea that everyone suffers? Is it something that you believe is true?

_____

_____

_____

Connor's therapist encouraged him to create a self-compassion script about the uncertainty he was facing in life. During their next session he gave her his script. It read:

_I'm really scared about all that may happen over the next several months. I'm going to need a lot of help from others._

*I don't know how being self-compassionate can help me right now, but I'm willing to try. Today I can be present with my emotional pain and allow myself to feel what I feel. I can sit with the sadness. I don't have to self-destruct.*

What do you think of Connor's self-compassion script? Do you have any ideas that you might add?

_____

_____

_____

_____

_____

Self-compassion as a mental health practice isn't designed to make everything better or take away justified and legitimate emotional pain. One self-compassionate act or listening to a self-compassion meditation will not undo decades of pain or make life better in just a few hours. Making that commitment to recovery requires a daily choice. My hope is that you will see that you are inherently worthy of that choice throughout your life.

Now, as you did at the beginning of the book, complete the following quiz to assess just how self-compassionate you are today. You can compare this with the quiz you took earlier to see how far you have come and what you can continue to work on. Feel free to retake this quiz every few months as you continue on your journey. This worksheet can also be found at http://www.newharbinger.com/55664.

## Quiz: How Self-Compassionate Are You?

Rate yourself on a scale of:

0 = this statement rarely or never applies to me

1 = this statement applies to me just a little

2 = this statement applies to me some of the time

3 = this statement applies to me about half the time

4 = this statement applies to me most of the time

5 = this statement almost always applies to me

I don't like myself a lot of the time.    _____

I experience self-disgust.    _____

I spend a lot of time blaming myself for problems that aren't always my responsibility.    _____

My friends have noticed that I'm really hard on myself.    _____

I demand a lot of perfection from myself.    _____

I call myself mean names when I'm alone.    _____

Self-acceptance seems more challenging for me than it is for others I know.    _____

I hate myself when I make mistakes.    _____

Sometimes I hurt myself when I think about things I've done or said in the past.    _____

It's hard for me to encourage myself.    _____

A family member, friend, teacher, or boss has said, "You should stop beating yourself up."    _____

I often imagine that I don't deserve happiness.    _____

I judge myself more than I judge others.    _____

It's rare for me to remember moments when I like myself or am proud of my accomplishments.    _____

When I'm self-critical, I tend to also be more critical of others.    _____

I get stuck imagining that my future is pretty hopeless.    _____

I spend a lot of time thinking that I should be more like other people.    _____

I cannot accept myself; I must change who I am.    _____

I frequently tell myself that I shouldn't feel the way that I do.    _____

If I say or do something in a group of people, I'll often want to "redo" what I said or did.    _____

Add up your total points along with today's date for future reference and reflection.

_____ points on _____.

A higher score (75 to 100 total points) indicates that you may have greater challenges in being self-compassionate. A score below 75 may indicate that you have low or moderate challenges in being self-compassionate and, of course, you still might have some room for improvement.

# Summary

- Terrible, horrible, no good, very bad days are a normal part of life.

- Everyday mistakes, missteps, and disappointments are an invitation to practice self-compassion.

- Your self-compassion practice will not make everything all better. It's not a "quick fix" or a one-size-fits-all solution to any mental health symptom or diagnosis.

- Being self-compassionate can alleviate some of your emotional pain.

- Suffering is common to all individuals at some point in their lives. You are not the exception.

- Self-compassion is a choice we make to help ourselves.

Add your own ideas below.

- _____

- _____

# Frequently Asked Questions and Answers About DBT and Self-Compassion

**Q.** Why are some people more self-compassionate than others? It looks like most people around me are pretty compassionate toward others as well as themselves. I've struggled with this as long as I can remember.

**A.** We don't necessarily know, but I have some ideas.

For some people, self-compassion may be more challenging because of how you were raised by parents or other caregivers. Some people were rarely encouraged to be self-compassionate as children and adolescents. The message they got growing up was, "You've got to be hard on yourself if you want to make good grades," or "Being nice to yourself is something for weak people. You aren't weak."

For others, practicing self-compassion may be extra challenging because of a diagnosis like depression, anxiety, PTSD, or borderline personality disorder. That's to say that the diagnosis may be an additional challenge even when the person wants to increase their capacity to be self-compassionate. Finally, emotionally sensitive individuals—with no mental health diagnosis—may also have a harder time being self-compassionate when their emotional experience feels intense or overwhelming.

No matter the cause, I'm a firm believer that self-compassion is something that can be learned and practiced. The goal is not to become a person who is perfectly self-compassionate at any given moment but to grow in greater self-compassion over time.

**Q.** I have a diagnosis of borderline personality disorder and also ADHD. Reading a lot of text is hard for me. I can't focus for long periods of time or my reading comprehension starts to fall apart. Do you have any suggestions for how to practice self-compassion that doesn't involve a lot of reading or writing?

**A.** Yes!

If you go to my website at hopeforbpd.com/self-compassion you can find several audio meditations and audio prompts that you can use at home or in the car. You'll find other helpful resources that may be beneficial too.

Be sure to check out the list of additional resources at the end of this book. You'll find a section on recommended podcasts and YouTube channels that may be helpful. Using a text-to-audio app on a phone or tablet can also make a difference for many people who struggle with reading for longer periods of time.

**Q.** These self-compassion ideas don't seem all that new or different from things I've heard from friends or my therapist. Isn't this just common sense?

**A.** Yes, I think that most of the ideas contained in this book are fairly self-explanatory or self-evident. You could absolutely say that they are "common sense."

Marsha Linehan has written about how the skills work when we really throw ourselves "all in" so that these ideas become a part of who we are and an integral part of how we conduct our lives. Even if the ideas aren't new to you, I'd love for you to ask yourself, "How can I make these techniques a part of my daily life—no matter what else is happening?"

Many of us feel inherently uncomfortable being self-compassionate, so we might practice a little here and a little there. That might be effective for many people, but for individuals who consistently struggle with their emotions, thoughts, and behaviors, they may need additional practice most days of the week.

Here's one more thought: Even ideas that are "common sense" can be very challenging. Becoming more self-compassionate may be one of the hardest things you ever do.

**Q.** I'm just not a self-compassionate person. Being nice to myself goes against all that I was taught growing up. It makes sense for me to encourage my friends to be self-compassionate because that's a part of my values, but it's hard to see how this is a fit for me. It feels fake and I don't want to be a fake person.

Is self-compassion really for everyone?

**A.** I absolutely understand your perspective.

Many people grew up in homes where self-compassion was actively discouraged. Even if you had parents, caregivers, teachers, or other role models who encouraged you to be kind toward yourself, it may have felt "wrong" or "bad." You may have even made decisions that were the opposite of self-compassionate and were actually self-harmful.

If you believe that self-compassion could be beneficial for other people, then why not you? Are you so different or unique that these ideas couldn't be helpful—even as you acknowledge that compassion or self-compassion benefits others?

Self-compassion is an important part of emotional health for everyone I've ever met. I want you to believe that you are worthy of healing. These ideas aren't just applicable to others. These ideas may also help you become the person you were meant to be.

Are you willing to challenge yourself and test to see whether these ideas could make a difference in your life? My hope is that you will say yes!

**Q.** Acceptance sounds like approval to me. Not only do I not like myself, but I also don't approve of the ways I've been hurt by others. Does that mean I can't use this skill?

**A.** Many people confuse acceptance with approval, so you are not alone.

Acceptance, however, does not mean that we like or approve of something that has been harmful to us or others. For instance, I can accept that I may be having a challenging day and may need to lean into some extra self-compassion as a way of coping with that challenging day, but I'm not saying that I like what is happening or approve of it.

I also encourage my therapy clients to think of acceptance as a choice they make to help themselves. Fighting reality may not help you feel better and may keep you stuck in unwanted thoughts and emotions.

Again, you get to decide how and when you use this skill. Marsha Linehan writes in her skills training manual (2015), "We can be a tulip in a rose garden." That might be true for you and could be another example of self-acceptance.

Could acceptance also help you become a more self-compassionate person? Maybe it's worth giving it a try to see whether it helps you.

**Q.** All of the distress tolerance skills make sense, but they are hard to remember. I can't remember them most of the time. How do people remember to use the STOP skill when urges come up?

**A.** I agree!

As a DBT therapist, this is one of the biggest struggles I see when I'm teaching the skills.

I often think about how teaching the skills is important, but consistently practicing the skills is what made the biggest difference for me when I was learning the skills. It's so important that I think it's also true for every DBT therapist I've ever met. We can't consistently use the skills if we don't commit to practicing the skills first. That practice helps us internalize the skills so that we can access them when we need them the most. Practice will help make the skills automatic, but it takes a lot of time.

Sometimes I'll ask my clients to practice using a skill like STOP every day for thirty days. That may seem like a lot of practice (and a pretty big commitment), but after that consistent practice, they'll see greater success using the skill. That success begets more success and people become more confident when they see how the skills help them help themselves.

DBT is very hard work. There's no substitute for daily practice. Today may be your day to start this life-changing practice.

# Resources

## YouTube Channels

BorderlinerNotes
youtube.com/@BorderlinerNotes

BPD Bunch
youtube.com/@thebpdbunch

Christopher Germer
youtube.com/@CenterforMindfulSelfCompassion

DBT Path
youtube.com/@DBTPath

Kristin Neff
youtube.com/@NeffKristin

## Websites

Amanda L. Smith, LCSW
mydialecticallife.com

hopeforbpd.com

Christopher Germer, PhD
chrisgermer.com

Emotions Matter
emotionsmatterbpd.org

Kristin Neff, PhD
self-compassion.org

# Mental Health, DBT, and Self-Compassion Podcasts

Evidence-Based: A New Harbinger Psychology Podcast
newharbinger.com/pages/podcast

The Happiness Lab Podcast
drlauriesantos.com/happiness-lab-with-dr-laurie-santos-podcast

Hidden Brain
hiddenbrain.org

The Science of Happiness
greatergood.berkeley.edu/podcasts/series/the_science_of_happiness

Self-Compassionate Professor
danielledelamare.com/subversive-self-compassion

# Instagram

instagram.com/christophergermerphd

instagram.com/neffselfcompassion/

# US and Canada-Based Nonprofit Organizations

Borderline Personality Disorder Association of British Columbia
bpdbc.ca

Borderline Personality Disorder Resource Center
bpdresourcecenter.org

Emotions Matter
emotionsmatterbpd.org

Florida Borderline Personality Disorder Association
fbpda.org

National Education Alliance for Borderline Personality Disorder
borderlinepersonalitydisorder.org

Sashbear
sashbear.org

# Memoirs and Biographies

Blauner, S. R. 2019. *How I Stayed Alive When My Brain Was Trying to Kill Me: One Person's Guide to Suicide Prevention.* New York: William Morrow.

Corso, D. 2017. *Stronger Than BPD: The Girl's Guide to Taking Control of Intense Emotions, Drama, and Chaos Using DBT.* Oakland, CA: New Harbinger Publications.

Van Gelder, K. 2010. *The Buddha and the Borderline: My Recovery from Borderline Personality Disorder Through Dialectical Behavior Therapy, Online Dating, and Buddhism.* Oakland, CA: New Harbinger Publications.

# Acknowledgments

Thank you:

To my clients, who are the bravest, coolest souls I'll ever know.

To David White, for being a calm husband and a gentle reader.

To Cheryl Honaker, for always being validating.

To Greg Brooks, for picking up the phone and saying funny things.

To Debbie DeMarco Bennett, for being a generous friend with compassionate wisdom.

To Kiera Van Gelder, for leading the good fight.

To the kind, exceedingly patient team at New Harbinger—Jess, Madison, Amy, Karen, and Callie—for creating beautiful, practical, and helpful books for all of us struggling through life.

Finally, to Marsha Linehan, for the inspiration to create a life worth living.

# References

APA (American Psychiatric Association). 2013. *Diagnostic and Statistical Manual of Mental Disorders.* 5th ed. Arlington, VA: APA.

Beaton, D. M., F. Sirois, and E. Milne. 2022. "The Role of Self-Compassion in the Mental Health of Adults with ADHD." *Journal of Clinical Psychology* 78 (12): 2497–2512.

Corso, D. 2017. *Stronger Than BPD: The Girl's Guide to Taking Control of Intense Emotions, Drama, and Chaos Using DBT.* Oakland, CA: New Harbinger Publications.

Germer, C. 2009. *The Mindful Path to Self-Compassion: Freeing Yourself from Destructive Thoughts and Emotions.* New York: Guilford Press.

Harned, M. 2022. *Treating Trauma in Dialectical Behavior Therapy: The DBT Prolonged Exposure Protocol (DBT PE).* New York: Guilford Press.

Kirschner, H., H. Kuyken, K. Wright, H. Roberts, C. Brejcha, and A. Karl. 2019. "Soothing Your Heart and Feeling Connected: A New Experimental Paradigm to Study the Benefits of Self-Compassion." *Clinical Psychological Science* 7 (3): 545–565.

Kramer, U., A. Pascual-Leone, K. B. Rohde, and R. Sachse. 2018. "The Role of Shame and Self-Compassion in Psychotherapy for Narcissistic Personality Disorder: An Exploratory Study." *Clinical Psychology and Psychotherapy* 25 (2): 272–282.

Linehan, M. M. 1993. *Cognitive-Behavioral Treatment of Borderline Personality Disorder.* New York: Guilford Press.

Linehan, M. M. 2015. *DBT Skills Training Manual.* 2nd ed. New York: Guilford Press.

Linehan, M. M. 2020. *Building a Life Worth Living: A Memoir.* New York: Guilford Press.

Liu, A., W. Wang, and X. Wu. 2020. "Understanding the Relation Between Self-Compassion and Suicide Risk Among Adolescents in a Post-Disaster Context: Mediating Roles of Gratitude and Posttraumatic Stress Disorder." *Frontiers in Psychology* 11: 1541.

May, G. 1982. *Will & Spirit: A Contemplative Psychology.* San Francisco, CA: Harper & Row.

Neff, K. 2011. *Self-Compassion: The Proven Power of Being Kind to Yourself.* New York: HarperCollins Publishers.

Sommerfeld, E., and M. S. Bitton. 2020. "Rejection Sensitivity, Self-Compassion, and Aggressive Behavior: The Role of Borderline Features as a Mediator." *Frontiers in Psychology* 11: 44.

Tali, E. E. S. Potharst, E. I. de Bruin, and E. M. W. J. Utens. 2023. "Self-Compassion and Anxiety in Adolescents with and without Anxiety Disorder." *Children* 10 (7): 1181.

Viorst, J. 1987. *Alexander and the Terrible, Horrible, No Good, Very Bad Day.* 2nd ed. New York: Atheneum Books for Young Readers.

**Amanda L. Smith, LCSW**, started out her career in mental health by serving as executive director of the Pinellas County, FL, affiliate of the National Alliance for Mental Illness (NAMI). In 2007, she founded the Florida Borderline Personality Disorder Association—a nonprofit organization dedicated to providing advocacy, education, and support for people diagnosed with borderline personality disorder (BPD) and their families. As a licensed clinical social worker, she provides comprehensive dialectical behavior therapy (DBT) services through her office in Waco, TX. She is also interested in evidence-based treatments like mentalization-based treatment and logotherapy. While she primarily works with individuals diagnosed with personality disorders, she is happy to meet with anyone who is open to finding more meaning and purpose in their life. You can reach her through her web site at www.hopeforbpd.com.

# MORE BOOKS from
# NEW HARBINGER PUBLICATIONS

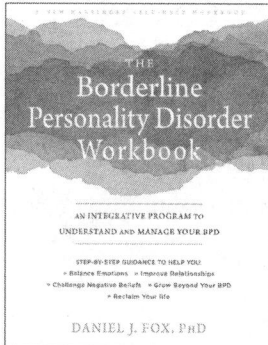

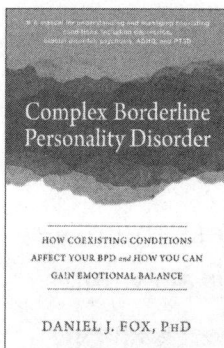

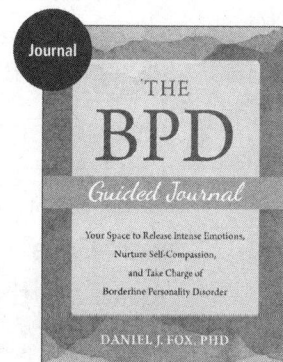

# Did you know there are **free tools** you can download for this book?

Free tools are things like **worksheets**, **guided meditation exercises**, and **more** that will help you get the most out of your book.

You can download free tools for this book— whether you bought or borrowed it, in any format, from any source—from the New Harbinger website. All you need is a NewHarbinger.com account. Just use the URL provided in this book to view the free tools that are available for it. Then, click on the "download" button for the free tool you want, and follow the prompts that appear to log in to your NewHarbinger.com account and download the material.

You can also save the free tools for this book to your **Free Tools Library** so you can access them again anytime, just by logging in to your account! Just look for this button on the book's free tools page.

**+ Save this to my free tools library**

If you need help accessing or downloading free tools, visit **newharbinger.com/faq** or contact us at **customerservice@newharbinger.com**.